Pra...
PRESENTATION
ESSENTIALS

Delivering an engaging presentation in person or virtually has never been more important, and Sardék and Anne's book helps all of us do just that with specific pragmatic steps to connect with any audience. *Presentation Essentials* is a must-read for all professionals looking to engage an audience with a message or story that inspires and compels action.

—**Tony Bingham,** CEO, Association for Talent Development

If you are looking to translate your ideas and passion into a presentation that will positively impact others, drive results, and earn impact, this is the book for you. The standards for capturing and holding others' attention have skyrocketed in recent years, so if you're not learning how to get better, you're already behind the curve. Two thumbs-up!

—**Caroline Adams Miller,** MAPP, professional speaker, executive coach, and *New York Times* bestselling author of *Creating Your Best Life, Getting Grit, My Name Is Caroline,* and *Positively Caroline*

Nothing will catapult your career like becoming a charismatic, engaging, and persuasive presenter. Bruce and Love provide the essential steps for self-transformation. The chapter on catchphrases and taglines alone is worth the price of the book!

—**Dianna Booher,** author of *Communicate with Confidence* and *Creating Personal Presence*

Presentation Essentials is not only a road map on how to structure your story to capture, engage, and inspire your audience, but also an in-depth guide on how to understand and calm your fears and play to your strengths, giving you the confidence and mindset to powerfully present yourself in a memorable way.

> —**Drew Gerber**, global CEO, Wasabi Publicity, Inc.

All you ever wanted to know about becoming a successful presenter, from grabbing your audience's attention to closing with pizzazz and everything in the middle, is all here! I have dozens of books on my shelf about this topic, and I could replace them all with this one book because it is loaded with practical tips, tools, and techniques that will make you a better presenter.

> —**Elaine Biech**, 2022 ISA Thought Leader and *Washington Post* bestselling author of *The Art and Science of Training*

Many people want to get "good" at presenting and speaking. This book will make you *great*. It is refreshing to see content that is not just a book of tips, but a real resource to supercharge your success with applications from start to finish.

> —**Shannon Wagers**, Fortune 50 Master Facilitator and North American talent development experience manager, Procter & Gamble

No matter how many presentations you've done, how long you've been presenting, what level you're at in your organization, or how often you present, you need to read this book. This is the single best resource to help you master presentations and take your career to the next level.

> —**Michael Sabbag**, director of leadership and organizational development, Broward Health

Whether you're a novice or seasoned pro, *Presentation Essentials* is like having a personal coach, on demand, to guide you through the process of planning, crafting, and delivering any type of presentation. Bruce and Love share their combined years of experience as professional speakers to provide a timely comprehensive resource that is authentic, insightful, and engaging.

—**Rita Bailey**, founder, Up To Something, LLC

Whether you are delivering a presentation in person or virtually, this book reveals, with stunning simplicity, the steps for captivating any audience. This is an absolute must-read for anyone who delivers presentations.

—**Timothy Howell**, chief people officer, Goodwill Industries of Northwest North Carolina

PRESENTATION
ESSENTIALS

PRESENTATION ESSENTIALS

THE TOOLS YOU NEED TO CAPTIVATE YOUR AUDIENCE, DELIVER YOUR STORY, AND MAKE YOUR MESSAGE MEMORABLE

ANNE BRUCE & SARDÉK LOVE

NEW YORK CHICAGO SAN FRANCISCO ATHENS LONDON
MADRID MEXICO CITY MILAN NEW DELHI
SINGAPORE SYDNEY TORONTO

1 2 3 4 5 6 7 8 9   LCR   27 26 25 24 23 22

ISBN   978-1-264-84251-3
MHID   1-264-84251-1

e-ISBN 978-1-264-84416-6
e-MHID   1-264-84416-6

Design by Mauna Eichner and Lee Fukui

McGraw Hill books are available at special quantity discounts to use as premiums and sales promotions or for use in corporate training programs. To contact a representative, please visit the Contact Us pages at www.mhprofessional.com.

McGraw Hill is committed to making our products accessible to all learners. To learn more about the available support and accommodations we offer, please contact us at accessibility@mheducation.com. We also participate in the Access Text Network (www.accesstext.org), and ATN members may submit requests through ATN.

We dedicate this book to the presenter inside each of us.

Contents

PART III
BEYOND THE ESSENTIALS

Acknowledgments

How fortunate am I? I simply string sentences together, and as a result I'm called an author, a coach, and a mentor. And to top it off, I'm privileged to walk among the most exceptional and selfless people on Earth.

McGraw Hill, yes you—one of the largest, most influential publishing entities in the world—you helped build my entire career—thank you. You've also helped me *Discover True North* (the title of one of my books you published, by the way). Donya Dickerson, associate publisher, you are a shining star. We've run across convention centers together, we've done countless book signings, and we've consoled one another in times of loss. Thank you for being one of my first brilliant editors. To Cheryl Segura, I continue to marvel at your exceptional talents as not only a senior editor but an avid supporter of authors like me. I love watching you rise as an editor, friend, daughter, wife, and mom. This is our second book together, and I've loved every minute of working with you. To Scott Sewell, senior marketing manager, I have learned so much from your publishing and marketing expertise, patience, and kindness. Thank you, friend. To the Eichner Fukui Design team—great job, once again. It's terrific working with you. You make the interior design of any book look stellar. And to Mark Morrow, one of my very first editors in this business. You made all the difference for me at the critical period between novice and writer. You continue to inspire and guide me. Thank you.

To Phyllis Jask. I believe all of the greatest accomplishments in life can be traced to the influences and extraordinary efforts and talents of others. This book is no exception. And every traceable step comes back to you. It has taken the extraordinary unconditional love and support of many wise and wonderful people to help me arrive at this author status. You have always made me feel like I have something valuable to say. It is one of the most remarkable gifts a person can receive. Thank you for the countless hours of wise and encouraging counsel and belief in me. I owe you a great debt. I love you dearly. We are family.

To my writing partner in all things truth—Sardék Love. We are two New Yorkers born a few miles from one another, and here today we are writing books together, giving presentations together, and talking and laughing on the phone all hours of the day and night. You're the brother I never had. I respect and admire you, and most of all, I appreciate your willingness to jump into wild and crazy projects with me (no questions asked), share your heart, and let me share mine. We're in this together, Sardék. You're a brilliant writer and a wonderful human being. Hurry up and come back to the beach soon . . . we've got a lot of promoting to do for future projects.

To my clients, I am thrilled to say you are also close friends. I'm a proud godmother and confidant to many of your children and family members. It's a grand privilege and honor. You know who you are. I appreciate you deeply, and I am humbled to be part of your extraordinary work.

Most of all to my intelligent, spiritual, compassionate, caring, and beautiful daughter, Autumn Kelly Bruce Mostovoj. Thank you for being born. You've opened my heart wider than I could ever have imagined possible. Thank you for always holding me in the light of your love, for your sound advice, and for your never-ending words of encouragement and devotion. You are forever my heart's wisdom and that is why I am a writer. I owe it all to you. I love you forever and ever.

And to my grandchildren, Nikolai and Noelle. You are my soul prints. You are my true north. Thank you for allowing me to be your *Grandma Fun*. Let the party begin!

If I have seen further it is by standing on the shoulders of giants.
—*Sir Isaac Newton*

—Anne Bruce

• • •

I was refining my DRIVE leadership model when I created a new law. The law of common ground says we grow together where we go together. It was the perfect statement as it reflects how organizations grow, how teams grow, and how I've grown. Success is never a lone wolf journey or a solo act, and this book would not be possible without the love and support from those whom I call my "growth team." I want to thank and honor them for their continued contributions as they have enabled me to continue to serve and support you.

I'll begin with Anne Bruce, my coauthor. Who knew a chance meeting on June 1, 2009, would transform my life? We've spoken on stages together. We've coached and mentored speakers and trainers together. And we've now written two books together. People always remember their firsts, and what makes Anne so remarkable is that she makes every moment of every interaction feel like it's the first. Thank you, Anne! You are a godsend, and I am honored to call you my dear friend.

To our editor, Cheryl Segura, and the entire team at McGraw Hill, I say thank you. It is with great honor I carry the prestigious badge of McGraw Hill author. To my wife, Thida Win-Love, and daughter, Latoshia Love, I thank you for your endless love and support. Finally, I want to thank all of my clients who supported the development of this book by allowing me to share their stories and examples. Your contributions to the lives of others will live on forever. I thank you.

—Sardék Love

Introduction

The mind is a wonderful thing. It starts to work the minute you are born and never stops until you get up to speak in public.
—**John Mason Brown,** literary critic

Whether you've never presented before or are an in-demand experienced keynoter, this book, *Presentation Essentials*, is going to help you improve, laugh out loud, and say to yourself, "Oh yeah, I can do that!"

We've had a blast writing this book together because we understand all of the feelings you can experience when it comes to speaking: the adrenalin rush, the fear, the dry mouth, the anxiety you're swept away in before you get up there, the confidence you feel after a successful presentation, and the sheer exhilaration of sharing your thoughts and ideas with others and seeing those light bulbs go off in the audience. Those "aha" moments you will witness and feel from your audiences (large or small) are worth a million dollars.

This book is not only a *how to do* a presentation type of book, it's also a *what to do* book for when you're preparing, when you make a mistake in front of everyone, when you need to understand and calm your fears. It includes ways to add zing to every presentation you deliver going forward—novice or seasoned presenter alike. This book is full of tips, tools, and techniques you need to captivate your audience, deliver your story with passion, and make your message more memorable and authentic. That's how success stories are born. It's how we build relationships. Solid gold presentations are essential for our present and future success, entrepreneurial startups, and million-dollar contracts. Presentations are also essential for everyday living. The truth is that almost every time we speak, we are presenting. Whether you're coaching your son or daughter in math, asking for a favor, explaining to your team what comes next in the big scheme of things, raising capital for your business, or putting your most charming self forward to ask for that date you've been wanting with someone special. It's all in the presentation!

In *Presentation Essentials* you'll find concise tips scattered throughout and two vital assessments you'll want to be part of and take over again after you've tried out our suggestions. We think they will help you to evaluate and chart your progress following each presentation you deliver or help others to sharpen their presentation skills, as well. In other words, this book contains valuable information you'll be able to refer to repeatedly as your presentation skill set develops, strengthens, and grows.

HOW TO USE THIS BOOK

This book is split into three distinct parts, each detailing important features that go into planning, crafting, and, finally, presenting your message. In Part I, "The Essentials," we break down what goes into a winning presentation. Chapter 1 covers how to overcome any hesitation you may be experiencing so you can concentrate on delivering a great presentation. In Chapter 2, you'll discover the fundamental structure to follow when creating your presentation. In Chapter 3, we discuss the different kinds of presentations and why you may need to make each one.

Part II, "The Essentials Applied," begins with a self-assessment for you to take inventory of your talents and strengths you now bring to the table. You'll also discover the challenges and new opportunities you'll want to improve on. This assessment is essential to all of the lessons in this book. It will help you calibrate your comfort zone, give you insights to what you enjoy and don't enjoy, and provide you with perspective on your various levels of presentation skills development.

Following the assessment, Chapter 4 explains the makeup of a powerful presentation and introduces the concept of the Big Idea Statement, the foundation on which your presentation is built. Next up is Chapter 5, which discusses storytelling and why it's so important. Chapter 6 examines presentation openers and why they are the make-or-break moments for you. Imagery plays a vital role in conveying a message of a presentation, and we cover this in Chapter 7. Chapter 8 reveals the secret weapon of a memorable presentation: the catchphrase or one-liner. In Chapter 9, we cover why you want to end your presentation with a memorable closer like a story or a powerful quote. In Chapter 10, we dive deep into delivering engaging and memorable online presentations. Chapter 11 focuses on helping you develop your individual signature style by channeling the best parts of your personality and amplifying them to leave a lasting impression on your audience. Wrapping up Part II is Chapter 12, which covers the fundamentals of presenting a formal speech.

Part III, "Beyond the Essentials," opens with Chapter 13, where we discuss the pros and cons of pursuing a career as a professional presenter. Chapter 14 talks more about establishing a relationship with the audience. We then close with our Presentation Essentials Toolkit, a collection of useful tips and tools we've developed to help you along your way to presentation greatness.

In our ordinary, everyday interactions—from the barista brewing our morning coffee to the parent-teacher conference we attend, and even all the way to those awesome and sometimes bizarre social media video clips we love to watch—we tell the world who we are by the way we present and share our ideas. Life is one big presentation, like it or not.

THE GIFT THAT KEEPS ON GIVING

If you break down the word "presentation," you'll clearly see the word "present," which is exactly what you should be giving your audience. Your message is your gift to the listener; whether you're informing, instructing, persuading, or entertaining, you are there to transmit information—our goal is to help you do that effectively, positively, and memorably.

And because life is all one giant performance, we're constantly being judged. In about three seconds or less, those on the receiving end of what we're saying are forming their first opinions of us, our competencies, and our capabilities to serve them or be a part of their decision-making process. It's human nature, and we all do it.

We rarely get a second chance to make that first impression. So it's very important to always be prepared and ready to grab every opportunity to make a positive impact on others, particularly with a planned presentation, demonstration, speech, or address. Nothing is more cringeworthy than a presentation that is not authentic; it's impersonal, untrustworthy, and fake, and above all it is a poor imitation of the real thing. Our emotional intelligence—our ability to form connections, have empathy for others, and be vulnerable and courageous—is what sets dynamic presenters apart from the rest and makes them the authentic deal to their audience.

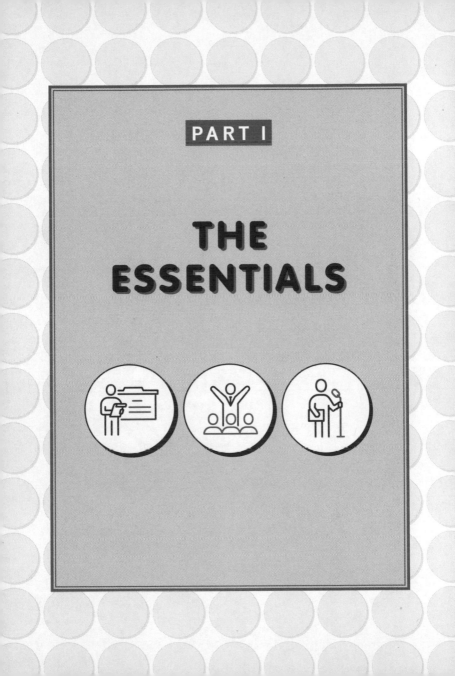

PART I

THE ESSENTIALS

From Overcoming Hesitation to Giving a Great Presentation

Great presenters are made, not born. Throughout this book, we're going to walk you through the "Essentials" of presentations, step-by-step and chapter by chapter. We'll give you the foundation you'll need to deliver a great presentation, from crafting a compelling opener to creating an audience-friendly, informative approach to ending with a powerful closing—and everything in between.

We begin with the truth that at some point in your business or personal life, you'll be asked to present some kind of information to an audience. It might be giving a persuasive speech at your child's PTA meeting or informing your work team about the latest government guidelines to follow. It requires courage to get in front of other people and share your message, which is why many people feel anxious when speaking or presenting in public. But they don't have to. With solid preparation, skill development, a generous helping of self-confidence, and some style, you can become a successful presenter—maybe even a pro.

When you nurture a set of skills—ones that you may already possess—and work on confidence-building techniques, you'll feel more prepared and less anxious about speaking in front of others. Once you've "trained your butterflies" (more on this later in this chapter), you can find your own unique way of connecting with your audience. And by "chunking down" your messages into influential bits, you'll not only be better equipped to remember your main points as you present, but you'll present in a way that allows your audience to easily remember your content.

Whether you're an introvert or extrovert, have delivered zero presentations or 100, or hate the idea of being in front of an audience, you can always improve and thrive. In fact, when we began our careers as professional presenters, we didn't have all the skills we needed. Instead, we developed and polished them over time, and you can, too!

DEVELOP ESSENTIAL PRESENTATION SKILLS

Presentation skills are the building blocks you'll use to construct and deliver your presentation.

Topping the list of valuable presentation skills are *authenticity* and *humility* because both establish your credibility with your audience. Always remember to be yourself and be natural. Almost anything else will come across as phony, false, and insincere. (Unless, of course, you're auditioning for a part in a movie, in which case go for it. Actors are presenters, too!) Developing your appeal and persona in an authentic way (via humor, a personal clothing style, or props, for instance) is a skill that will help you remain memorable and

4

marketable. By using your signature presentation style, discussed in-depth in Chapter 11, you'll connect with an audience and influence how successfully your message is communicated.

Armed with other important skills, such as *good verbal communication, annunciation* (projecting your voice), and *articulation* (speaking clearly), you'll deliver a memorable message with confidence and clarity. Try not to mumble—instead, be proud that you have a valuable contribution to share. *Strong nonverbal communication* skills, such as body language, facial expressions, and how you move (or don't move), all influence how relatable you appear to your audience.

A little *self-confidence* will help if you are nervous about speaking in front of others. Believe in yourself and be confident that you have been tasked with presenting because you know your content. Your confidence will show in your body language and stance. Remember, your audience wants you to succeed, too.

Using a distinct voice can be appealing to your audience as well. Some of the most memorable presenters, like the late Gilbert Gottfried or comedian Bobcat Goldthwait, have unusual and distinct voices that separate them from the pack. If your voice is an asset you'd like to develop, work with coaches who specialize in speech and voice.

Self-awareness and *emotional intelligence* aren't necessarily skills, but they are useful and important tools a presenter should develop. If you're presenting in front of an audience, keep calm and cool, especially when confronted with a difficult audience, a technology failure, a stage malfunction, or any number of unexpected issues that may appear during a presentation. The goal of presenting is being able to communicate your message in a clear and compelling way, regardless of any obstacles you may encounter.

Armed with these skills, a dash of quick thinking, and a sprinkle of showmanship, you'll be presenting like a pro in no time.

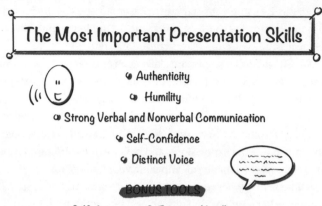

The Most Important Presentation Skills

- Authenticity
- Humility
- Strong Verbal and Nonverbal Communication
- Self-Confidence
- Distinct Voice

BONUS TOOLS

Self-Awareness & Emotional Intelligence

HOW TO TRAIN YOUR BUTTERFLIES

Earlier we mentioned "training your butterflies." Before getting to the how-to, it's important to know that everyone gets that fluttering deep in the gut or that nervousness when anxious—and some feel that especially when giving a presentation. There's even a word for fear of public speaking: *glossophobia*. While this may be true, any excessive nervousness you feel or show can be distracting to your audience. Signs of nervousness include fidgeting with your hands, spinning a pen, touching yourself too much, constantly running your fingers through your hair, always clearing your throat, excessive blinking, swallowing a lot, tapping a pencil, saying "um" or "uh" after every sentence (that's the most distracting), and your hands shaking.

To understand where you are on your presentation journey right now, take time to list those signs that make you appear nervous.

My Current Nervous Habits

Once you've identified what makes you look nervous, use that awareness to address and eliminate these habits. Here are a few nerve-controlling tips to start that process:

- Film yourself speaking.

- Ask someone for candid feedback after you present. (There is a Postpresentation Evaluation in the Presentation Essentials Toolkit at the end of the book, so keep reading!)

- Be prepared. The more prepared you are the less nervous you will be.

- If you're using notes, number the pages in case you drop them.

- Visit your presentation environment early so that you get a feel for the room ahead of time.

- Wear comfortable clothes and shoes. Try these on in advance to make sure everything fits properly and you can move your body as needed.

- If you're using a mic, do a sound check. If an audiovisual person is involved, meet or talk with that person beforehand.

- Practice positive self-talk before delivering a speech. We'll get you started: *You've got this!*

- Sleep, eat, breathe. Get rest beforehand, eat something light (low blood sugar doesn't help the nerves), and do breathing exercises. Meditate and gather your thoughts privately before showtime. (Deep breathing just five times slowly—in through your nose and exhaling from your mouth—puts five times more oxygen in your brain. That alone can calm nerves in a hurry.)

- Breath control is critical. Stop between sentences and breathe.

- Search online for and experiment with different relaxation techniques that may work for you. Everyone is different. Some presenters exercise or run before a speech. Others stretch or do yoga.

- When talking or thinking about your upcoming presentation, replace the word "nervous" with "excitement" or "anticipation." Sometimes the word itself triggers nervousness.

Any or all of these tips can have a powerful, calming effect, so test them to find your best solution.

HARNESS THE POWER OF CONNECTIVITY

Now that you have tips for controlling your nerves, let's tackle connecting with your audience. A major part of giving a presentation is knowing and connecting with the people in front of you (in person or on a screen—or both) through not only your words, but your gestures, the visual aids you use, and even what you wear.

How do you connect with your audience in the moment, even if you're a tad apprehensive? First think about this: Are you present in the moment, or are your thoughts elsewhere? It doesn't matter the size of your audience—it can be a very large gathering or just a one-on-one conversation. You want to leave a memorable and long-lasting impression, and you achieve this through connectivity and emotional intelligence. Put yourself in the shoes of your listener, audience, or client and ask yourself what you like best and least regarding your interaction.

A great way to do this is to ask yourself these questions:

- **What specific things do you do personally to connect with others that you have found particularly effective?** Do you make eye contact? Do you mention people specifically by name? Do you warmly smile and try to make each person feel like he or she is the only one you're speaking to? People are compelled to listen to friendly people.

- **When you are presenting an idea and there is a disagreement, conflict, or confrontation, how do you handle it?** How do you defuse a "hot" encounter? Have you ever tried using appropriate humor to lighten the situation?

- **What do you like best about presentations you've attended?** What makes you look forward to someone's presentation?

- **What do you like least about presentations you've attended?** What bores you or makes you dread the interaction?

- **What do you enjoy about certain conference or video calls?** What gives you anxiety—being on camera, being scrutinized by peers, or answering questions on the spot?

- **Do you consider audience demographics when crafting a presentation?** Knowing audience demographics, including age, income, and gender, can influence how you present your information through the words you choose, any kind of cultural or pop culture references you use to relate to them, and more.

- **Do you think about psychographics such as attitudes (your audience's emotions or beliefs about a subject) and aspirations (their hopes or goals) and their impact on your presentation?** How does your perception of your audience drive ultimate outcomes and build long-lasting relationships?

- **Have you considered what impact your written communication has on your credibility as a presenter?** Even though presentations are primarily delivered through speaking, many include a chat function or visual aids with writing. How articulately you present yourself in writing during a presentation can alter how your audience perceives you. If your slides contain spelling errors, for example, it affects your credibility and how your audience assesses your expertise.

Asking yourself these questions helps establish a connection with your audience. It's vital for a presenter to convey warmth, personality, knowledge, and good humor (digitally, in-person, or virtually) in order to effectively communicate a message. Thinking through these questions will help you do exactly that.

CHUNKING IT DOWN WITH THE METHOD OF THREE

You've probably never heard someone in an audience say, "Gee, I wish that presenter had gone on and on." Which leads us to the next secret to a winning presentation: chunking it down.

Audiences are hardwired for immediate gratification and instant information, so you'll be most successful if you keep your presentation short and use the Method of Three: build the core of your message with just three main points. Three tends to be the magic number for what people can easily understand, take away, and apply. It also makes it easier to memorize and recall a presentation—especially when those butterflies flutter. Focusing on main points puts you in the right headspace to deliver your message. By chunking things into threes, you unify, explain, and strengthen your ultimate message. Here are some examples:

- **Sales meeting.** Here are three ways to underscore this product's features and benefits to the customer.

- **Training session.** Teach-back (see Chapter 3) three things that your team learned after you come back from the break.

- **Eulogy.** The three main reasons my life has been changed forever because of Billy are . . .

- **Toast.** Happy birthday, Mom! These are the three biggest life-changing lessons you taught me growing up.

- **Roast.** Select two jokes or humorous stories about the person being roasted and then support the conclusion with why none of that is real and here's why.

- **Monday morning briefing for the team.** The top three goals we want to achieve today in order of priority are . . .

Chunking down a message into threes will help make things clear and memorable—for both the presenter and audience. It also automatically underscores the purpose of the presentation.

REMINDER:

Build the core of your
message using the
Method of Three.

HOW TO LOSE YOUR AUDIENCE IN FIVE EASY STEPS

Now that you know the starting "dos" for presenting, let's spin things around and tell you how *not* to present. You'll thank us when you don't do any of these:

1. **Demonstrate zero energy.** Take a note from Ben Stein's performance as the economics teacher in the iconic movie

Ferris Bueller's Day Off and do not be boring, monotonous, repetitive, lackluster, or generally uninspiring. We're falling asleep just thinking about it. Good presenters are appropriately energetic and effectively demonstrate why they want to share their message.

2. **Lurk behind the lectern.** Never hide behind or lean on the lectern or podium when presenting on a stage. Instead, realize the lectern is there to hold your notes or the mic, not your leaning elbow. Step away from the podium to make a point. Heck, get out there and walk around to engage your audience! They'll love you for it.

3. **Deliver death by slide deck.** Don't fill your presentations with too many slides, too much text, no main point, bad graphics, and multiple competing fonts. Don't read everything on the slide to your audience. Avoid droning on and on or risk burying your message and losing your audience's interest. (More on this in Chapter 7.)

4. **Be a talking head.** Reading your presentation word-for-word from prepared index cards—sloppily written for better effect—is a huge *no*. You risk losing your place and looking foolish to your audience. Good presenters know the essence of their message and how they want to say it—and if they lose their place or miss a point, they smoothly backtrack to catch their audience up. Remember the Method of Three.

5. **Be disingenuous.** When you start off by appearing inauthentic, desperate, or overly confident and cocky, you're bound to have an effect—a *bad one*! This is the kind of

presenter audiences love to hate. Conversely, when you are authentic and present with warmth and humility, audiences relate to you and are more apt to listen to your message. Greet people as they enter the room. Shake hands. Introduce yourself and take names—then really try to remember those names. There's nothing more appealing than a presenter who looks at an audience member and says, "John told me earlier he too had experienced this situation last month." Relatability (and connecting with people on a basic human level) is everything.

• • •

Even if the thought of presenting fills you with anxiety, rest assured you can develop presentation skills and tame your butterflies so you can connect with your audience. You can deliver your message with confidence and clarity with the dos, don'ts, tips, and tricks in this chapter and other chapters throughout this book.

ESSENTIAL TAKEAWAYS

At the end of each chapter, you'll find Essential Takeaways. These are the most important points you'll need to carry into your professional and personal lives to find lasting success. In this chapter, the Essential Takeaways are:

- Anyone can develop and practice good presentation skills.

- Audience connection is vital to your believability, credibility, and relatability.

- Remember to use the Method of Three when developing your main point.

- Control presentation nerves by recognizing what triggers your anxieties and work to remedy those triggers.

CHAPTER

2

Presentation Structure

We've all heard the statement, "Every presentation has a beginning, middle, and end." Yet when creating a presentation, that truthful statement fails to provide any meaningful guidance. Often people are stuck trying to figure out where to begin and what to say. If you want to captivate your audience, deliver your story, and make your message memorable, begin with your presentation structure.

Fortunately, the human mind is attracted to a story because we describe our life experiences in story format. Great presenters use this to their advantage, and you can too because stories create a structure that provides a wide array of proven tools for crafting highly effective presentations. Once you know the process to create a presentation, you'll never again be stuck wondering where to begin or what to say.

NEVER START CREATING A PRESENTATION BY ASKING THIS QUESTION

When creating a presentation, most people start by asking, "What am I going to say?" The problem with starting with this question is twofold: First, it leads you to the realization that you have too much to say with too little time to say it. Second, the answer leads you to try to say it all anyway. That's a surefire recipe for presentation disaster.

Instead, the most effective question to ask when beginning to prepare your presentation is, "What is the key point I wish to make?" By answering that question, you are defining what's known as the Big Idea. From there, all the remaining elements of an effective presentation structure fall into place like pieces of a puzzle.

Let's review the three pillars of presentation structure and then dive deeper into each.

THREE PILLARS OF PRESENTATION STRUCTURE

To captivate your audience, create the skeletal outline of your presentation using this structure:

- **Pillar 1: The Situation.** This is where the presenter defines the problem being addressed, creates a statement to motivate the audience to take action after the presentation, and identifies what's at stake if the audience fails to take action.

- **Pillar 2: Building the Case for Change.** Here the presenter builds the case for change by making one to three key points that challenge the status quo.

- **Pillar 3: The Better Future and Call to Action.** Finally, the presenter defines a better future and appeals for a call to action.

Let's explore each pillar to see how to properly construct it with ease.

Pillar 1: The Situation

When invited to deliver a presentation, we're typically given a topic to address. Before you begin developing the presentation, it is critically important to establish what your audience is currently experiencing with respect to that topic.

Every audience expects your presentation to add value to them by providing ways to improve their current situation and make their lives better. By establishing and understanding what they are currently experiencing, you set the stage for building a compelling case for change and inviting the audience to take a very specific action toward a better future.

Establishing the situation requires you to ask a series of questions to construct what's known as your presentation's Big Idea. If you want to be compelling, defining your Big Idea is where it all begins.

The Big Idea Statement

So, what's the Big Idea anyway? That is the central question you need to answer to understand the situation at hand. Before designing your presentation, you must create your Big Idea Statement. The Big Idea Statement is the main point of your presentation, and its purpose is to compel your audience to reconsider what they know to be true and take action to change. The Big Idea Statement contains three components:

1. **The problem** your audience faces.

2. **Your expert insights** for overcoming the problem.

3. **The stakes** involved.

Crafting this powerful statement relies on limiting your Big Idea to just one desire your audience has. Here is how to form each component of your Big Idea Statement.

Big Idea Statement Part 1: The Problem

Finding the "right" problem to address in your presentation can seem daunting when, with any given subject, there are so many potential options to choose from. The secret to selecting the "right" problem is to follow this simple, failproof process:

- **Step 1: Ask yourself, "What problems does your audience have that meet all three of these criteria?"**

  - The problem is urgent.

  - The problem is widespread.

  - The problem is expensive.

Take five minutes to brainstorm a list of potential problems you can help solve and capture them using the problem severity matrix shown at the end of this section. You can use this matrix as a framework for your own real-life issues.

- **Step 2: Rank the list of problems.** Rank each problem in your brainstormed list based on your perceived level of severity using a scale of 1–5, with 1 being low severity and 5 being high severity.

- **Step 3: Choose the most severe problem to address.** The fact is, a problem that meets all three criteria and ranks high on your severity scale is a massive problem for your audience. This is true because the longer the problem remains unresolved, the higher the probability the person or team responsible for finding a solution to the problem will be reassigned, replaced, or terminated. So, your message is crucial in their success and your presentation should inspire them to take action.

For training professionals who may be developing multiple presentations covering a wide array of topics, the problem selection process may not appear to be applicable to them. In reality, this is exactly what will make your training incredibly compelling and transferrable on the job.

Remember to always follow the mantra *only include content that moves them closer to attaining their goal* as you develop your Big Idea. If it doesn't make a measurable, positive difference, it doesn't deserve to take up valuable time and space in your presentation.

If you're stuck on what would qualify as a "problem" when you're working on your presentation, here are a few examples of problems we've addressed in our presentations:

- More than 40 percent of employees are planning to leave your organization in the next six months.

- More than 50 percent of your virtual training content is a complete waste of time, money, and resources.

- More than half of your leaders are ill-equipped to lead hybrid teams in a postpandemic world.

Sample Problem Severity Matrix

The Problem	Severity Rating (1 being low and 5 being high)
More than 40 percent of employees are planning to leave your organization in the next six months.	
More than 50 percent of your virtual training content is a complete waste of time, money, and resources.	
More than half of your leaders are ill-equipped to lead hybrid teams in a postpandemic world.	

Big Idea Statement Part 2: Your Expert Insights

To persuade others to take action, a presenter must persuade the audience members to reconsider what they believe to be true. This requires creating moments of surprise, which most people call "aha" moments. These are the moments where you find yourself saying statements like, "I did not know that!" or "Wow!" or "That is really cool!" Screenwriters, authors, and marketers call these moments the Moment of Truth for good reason. They are the launching point from which the audience realizes what they thought to be true is false.

By creating this gap in the mind of the audience, that incongruence serves as a great motivator to take action because humans want to keep our world orderly and predictable. This is where your expertise and unique insights come into play. When developing your Big Idea, use your expertise and unique insights to create a statement that challenges the audience's current perspectives, knowledge, and beliefs.

Apple cofounder Steve Jobs was famous for creating hugely successful moments of truth during product launches. In fact, three-time *Wall Street Journal* bestselling author Carmine Gallo shared the perfect example of Jobs's expertise and unique insights in action during the launch of the first iPod:

> When Steve Jobs introduced the first iPod, he told the audience that the music player could store 1,000 songs. While other music players on the market could make the same claim, Jobs explained that none of the competitors' devices could fit in your pocket. And with the flair of a magician pulling a rabbit out of his hat, Jobs reached into the pocket of his jeans and pulled out the smallest MP3 player on the market. *One thousand songs in your pocket* became one of the most iconic taglines in product history.[1]

That single phrase—"one thousand songs in your pocket"—was simply brilliant because it profoundly challenged what people thought to be true. You can leverage the power of a simple formula to create the same magical "aha" moments in your Big Idea Statement and presentations. The formula for creating "aha" moments is:

Everybody thinks X, but what is actually true is Y.

Let's put Steve Jobs's iPod launch phrase into the formula and you'll easily see why it worked so well:

Everybody thinks X (storing 1,000 songs requires a
large piece of hardware), but what is actually true is Y
(the hardware can fit in your pocket).

Let's look at three more examples of this in action. We'll use the three problems we wanted to solve in Big Idea Part 1: The Problem. The italic text shows the expert insights we've added to solve the original problem:

- More than 40 percent of employees are planning to leave your organization in the next six months *because your managers fail to do this one thing*.

- More than 50 percent of your virtual training content is a complete waste of time, money, and resources, *leaving team members unprepared to fulfil their job duties*.

- More than half of your leaders are ill-equipped to lead hybrid teams in a postpandemic world, *and your competitors are actively poaching the 30 percent of your leaders who do*.

Big Idea Statement Part 3: The Stakes

The final piece of the Big Idea Statement focuses on the stakes involved. The stakes—which we define as the risk of failure if the audience does not take action—are critical. These stakes motivate your audience to take action. For example, if a company doesn't get additional funding in 30 days, it could go out of business. Going out of business would be the stakes in that scenario. You've properly defined the stakes for your audience when the stakes would make inaction impossible on their behalf.

To uncover the stakes for your presentation, answer the question, "What negative outcome does my audience have a strong desire to avoid?" Plug that answer into your Big Idea Statement for a compelling thesis and a solid foundation for building your presentation.

Let's look back to those three examples we've been building on so far and wrap things up by adding the stakes to each:

- **Example 1**

  o **The Problem:** More than 40 percent of employees are planning to leave your organization in the next six months.

  o **Your Expert Insights:** because your managers fail to do this one thing

  o **The Stakes:** it will destroy your profitability

  o **The Big Idea Statement:** More than 40 percent of employees are planning to leave your organization in the next six months because your managers fail to do this one thing, and it will destroy your profitability.

- **Example 2**

  o **The Problem:** More than 50 percent of your virtual training content is a complete waste of time, money, and resources.

  o **Your Expert Insights:** leaving team members unprepared to fulfil their job duties

  o **The Stakes:** putting your human capital investment dollars at severe risk

  o **The Big Idea Statement:** More than 50 percent of your virtual training content is a complete waste of time, money, and resources, leaving team members unprepared to fulfil their job duties, thereby putting your human capital investment dollars at severe risk.

- **Example 3**

  o **The Problem:** Over half of your leaders are ill-equipped to lead hybrid teams in a postpandemic world.

  o **Your Expert Insights:** your competitors are actively poaching

  o **The Stakes:** the 30 percent of your leaders who do

  o **The Big Idea Statement:** Over half of your leaders are ill-equipped to lead hybrid teams in a postpandemic world, and your competitors are actively poaching the 30 percent of your leaders who do.

As you can see, the Big Idea is a powerful tool for laying the building blocks of an incredibly compelling presentation. Now that you've seen the Big Idea process in action, let's do a brief review.

You start constructing your Big Idea Statement by defining the "right" problem to address—one that is urgent, widespread, and expensive if left unresolved. Next, use your expertise and unique insights to create a Big Idea Statement that challenges the audience's current perspectives, knowledge, and beliefs. Finally, plug in a negative outcome that the audience should have a strong desire to avoid.

By putting all three of those components together, you have created a solid foundation from which to build a captivating presentation. Here is a fantastic example of former Ford CEO Alan Mulally putting the Big Idea in action:

Alan Mulally was set to begin his first press conference as the newly hired CEO of Ford Motor Company. In the room were 400 journalists, with an additional 1,400 attending virtually. Alan was a successful aerospace engineer who came to Ford after serving many years in manufacturing executive roles with Boeing. What was notable about his hiring was that he was the first leader in the history of the global automotive industry to lead a major manufacturer who had no prior automotive industry experience.

As the press conference got underway, one journalist said, "With all due respect Mr. Mulally, the automobile business is very, very complex, starting with the products themselves. Since you don't know anything about the business or the vehicles, what does that mean to us? That we're in trouble and we have you here?" Alan rubbed his chin thoughtfully and said, "Well, I really do agree with you that the automobile industry is very sophisticated starting with the products. Matter of fact, an average car or truck has around 10,000 parts. When you think about the engineering, the manufacturing, and the aerodynamics and the system integration, they are very, very sophisticated products. I might point out that the Boeing 777 airplane has four million parts, and it stays in the air." The next day, the *Detroit News* ran a headline that stated: "I Think We Got the Right Guy."[2]

Alan had an incredible response. He knew what all exceptional presenters know and did the work before his presentation to create an impactful Big Idea Statement.

By comparing a 10,000-part ground-based vehicle to a four-million-part aircraft that must stay airborne, he masterfully created a memorable "aha" moment in his response to the journalist using his expert insights from years of experience as an engineering executive with Boeing. He proved a leader from outside the automotive industry could lead and succeed because he helped Ford beat bankruptcy and returned the company to financial stability.

• • •

Once you craft your Big Idea Statement, you're ready to construct a powerful presentation. This is done by building the case for change.

The Big Idea Statement

Definition:

The main point of your presentation. Its purpose is to compel your audience to reconsider what they know to be true and take action to change.

Includes 3 parts:

- The Problem
- Expert Insights
- The Stakes

Pillar 2: Building the Case for Change

Congratulations! You've established the situation by sharing your Big Idea Statement. Now it's time to build the case for the audience to change, and the majority of your presentation will be dedicated to building this case. Just like a movie building to a climactic scene, you'll make your case for your audience to (take action to) change by repeatedly sharing examples that ultimately make inaction impossible. When creating the case for change is done properly, the stage is set to invite your audience to take action—the final step in crafting a compelling presentation.

To build the case for change, you must begin chipping away at the status quo by highlighting how the problem is wreaking havoc on your audience. Typically, the case for change is constructed using three key points that expose and amplify the problem the audience wants to overcome. Making the case for change follows a three-act story structure, a very familiar pattern for most audiences.

Case for Change Part 1: The Struggle

A large global mining organization ramped up its focus on safety after several incidents in the global industry exposed significant vulnerabilities in long-standing operational practices. A consultant team led by John had completed phase I of the safety culture assessment project, and the team's findings and recommendations were being delivered to senior leadership.

They began their assessment in the US operations and then proceeded to the African operations in Liberia before concluding with operations in the Siberian city of Kemerovo, Russia. As part of their standard practice, the consulting team observed the operations in action. John began the senior leadership presentation by sharing the findings for operations in West Virginia.

It was a brisk spring day when the team toured the US operations, and shortly after arriving, John and his team took a brief walking tour inside a newly cut mine. They immediately noticed structural deficiencies in the ceiling that, if left unresolved, could lead to a ceiling collapse. The team quickly retreated out of the mine, and when asked about the deficiencies, the local safety leader's response was, "I guess the guys may have been a little lazy when working that day." It was frighteningly clear to John and his team they were facing a gargantuan uphill battle to help the company improve safety. As he put it, "It's not just that the employees in the West Virginia operations are working in unsafe conditions. It's that their leaders don't care about them enough to ensure they work safely." That was a crushing statement for the senior leaders to hear.

John used the findings from his team's observations to establish the existence of the problem, and then he proceeded to describe the problem in very stark (and in this case very chilling) terms.

In your presentation, follow the same presentation framework. After identifying the problem, quickly pivot to expose the struggle it creates for your audience. Now on to Part 2: The Conflict.

Case for Change Part 2: The Conflict

John continued his presentation by sharing the findings from Liberia, one of the poorest countries in the world. The United Nations still had an armed presence to maintain the peace after the country had suffered through more than 12 brutal years of two civil wars. The wars were so devastating that roads did not exist, and it was an understatement to say that traveling by car to the multiple locations was rife with unusually high safety risks. Despite this, the Liberian operations' safety incident rates were astonishingly good with one huge exception. The raw materials transfer operations were dealing with safety issues that led to a ship being improperly loaded, and it ran aground before it could leave the shallow waters of the port. John noted the Liberians were incredibly proud and hard workers. The problem was more insidious. They lacked proper equipment, so they were forced to improvise. As one worker put it, "If there's a way, we have the will." In his presentation,

John told the senior executives, "Give these people the proper way so that they can work safely at will."

John had exposed a new villain—a lack of equipment—to drive home the need for change. He knew the senior leaders were motivated to invest in Liberia because the company had built schools in several local communities as part of the international effort to rebuild the country and improve the quality of life. Notice how John built upon his first main point—"leaders don't care"—to "caring leaders" being the source of a better future.

In your presentation, identify the next problem that exists for your audience. Tell a short story to illuminate the presence of the problem, and if possible, explain how the problem makes things just a bit worse for them. By doing this, you are effectively building the case for your audience to consider taking action based on your recommendation in your call to action.

Case for Change Part 3: The Conflict Continues

In this final point, address yet another significant problem your audience would like to eliminate, avoid, or minimize. And once again, tell a short story to expose the problem followed by a brief explanation of how you, your product, or your service is the solution to the problem.

Now you are ready to close your presentation, and that is done in Pillar 3.

Pillar 3: The Better Future and Call to Action

Now that the case for change has been constructed, it's time to paint a picture of a better future for your audience and invite them to take the action necessary to achieve the future you describe in this final pillar.

John moved to the next phase of his presentation by explaining how he and his team unexpectedly discovered a stunningly effective best practice in the least likely of places—Kemerovo, Russia. Local management hung photographs of miners' children from the ceiling of the hallway that led to the entrance to the underground mine. On each photo was a personal statement from the child (or children) appealing to their dad to work safe and come back home. As each miner walked down the hallway, he would look up just once—at his children's photo—and continue. Observing this, John instantly inquired about it and was told the mine posted those photos five years prior and their safety record has been near 100 percent ever since. The simple act of posting the children's photos led John to share a heartwarming story that tugged at a caring senior leadership team. It was a brilliant move. John then shared three recommendations and invited the leaders to make a choice—the obvious choice being to take action—to improve the safety for their employees.

To close your presentation, follow the same structure. Paint a picture of a better future. Don't leave this to chance or open to interpretation. Be explicit in stating how the audience's world will be better. After creating the vision of a better world, tell them what you want to do. State your call to action. Be brief. It's really that simple.

Follow this three-pillar structure and you'll create a presentation that keeps your audience interested and open to take action based on your superbly constructed presentation.

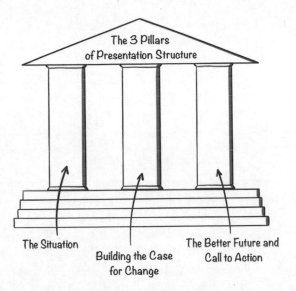

The 3 Pillars of Presentation Structure

The Situation

Building the Case for Change

The Better Future and Call to Action

ESSENTIAL TAKEAWAYS

- Structuring a presentation helps to captivate your audience, deliver your story, and make your message memorable.

- Don't ask yourself, "What am I going to say?" Instead, ask, "What is the key point I wish to make?"

- Identify the three pillars of your presentation structure by establishing the situation, building the case for change, and defining a better future with a call to action.

- Identify the problem or issue to address, rank its severity, and choose the most severe as the focus of your presentation.

The Different Types of Presentations

No matter what type of presentation you're giving, your goal is to inform, instruct/educate, entertain, or persuade your audience to solve a challenge, concern, or problem. There are various types of presentations you may do, either in your role as a professional or in your personal life (e.g., as a volunteer or parent). In this chapter, we break down presentations into three categories: training, business, and nonbusiness. Of course, overlaps exist across these categories, but each presentation has a purpose and intent.

Let's start by understanding why you might need to give a presentation.

REASONS FOR GIVING A PRESENTATION

What do the following people have in common?

- The waiter at your favorite restaurant describes to you and everyone at your table the daily chef's specials.

- A loved one at a wedding toasts the newly married couple or the best man recounts stories of childhood pranks.

- A teacher presents to a classroom of students in a way that makes history or algebra interactive and exciting.

- An IT team unveils a new content management system, hoping for an increased budget next year and new hire approval.

- A PTA volunteer running a school fundraiser explains to parents via a video call the positive outcomes they can expect for their children.

- A development director tries to land a new benefactor.

- An airline supervisor presents ways to improve processes and efficiency for a ground operations team, hoping to increase hiring budgets in the next fiscal year.

While all of these people are presenters, their reasons for presenting vary greatly and each is addressing a specific purpose and audience. Chances are you too will be required to present something at some point in your life.

There are typically four main reasons to present information: to *inform (sometimes referred to as the pitch)*, to *instruct or educate*, to *entertain*, and to *persuade*. Your reasons for presenting will fall under these categories too. In the previous examples, the reasons for giving a presentation usually fall into one of these four categories:

- The waiter informs the diners what is available or the night's special.

- The loved one or friend entertains at a wedding or in a conversation.

- The teacher, IT team, and airline supervisor instruct, but also persuade. They may also be pitching an idea for the benefit of the group.

- The PTA volunteer and the development director persuade and influence.

Just as the reasons for delivering a presentation vary, so do the situations requiring a presentation. In your professional and personal lives, you may be asked to give different types of presentations.

BUSINESS PRESENTATIONS

Because most of this book focuses on business presentations, we'll keep this section brief. Although presenting may not be on your job description, you'll likely have to present at least once in your career, so let's get you started on that path.

At its heart, every presentation should have a solid beginning, a middle with main points chunked out into memorable bits, great and engaging visuals, an unforgettable one-liner or catchphrase, and an impactful close. The "why" behind your business presentation is going to be much like any other: inform, instruct/educate, or persuade. (We're leaving out "entertain" unless you're a comedian or humorist.)

A business presentation isn't that much different from a training or nonbusiness presentation—you're still creating a strong presentation to get your message out. What sets it apart is that you often already possess a strong knowledge of your audience because it may be made up of your colleagues (e.g., if you're an HR professional informing your teams about the latest benefits packages, or you're the in-house counsel explaining the newest compliance measures). Because your audience probably knows the business atmosphere and culture, you may already feel connected to them—and that's always a plus when presenting. It puts you at ease and helps you feel more confident as you present. And, of course, a business presentation is typically going to affect business operations or processes, which is why it needs to be given in the first place.

TRAINING PRESENTATIONS

What's the significant difference between training and a general business presentation? And why are we specifically setting training apart from other presentation types? This is frequently a source of confusion. Training is presenting, but primarily concentrates on audience outcomes; training and presenting require similar skills, but there are very clear and important differences. This table identifies the five main differences between presenting and training.

Presenting Versus Training

	Presenting	Training
Purpose	Get a message across	Improve participant performance
Source of Expertise	The presenter	Shared between the presenter and the participant(s)
Focus	Information sharing	Skill development
Audience Involvement	Both passive and interactive	Active and continuous
Primary Tools Used	Rhetorical questions and storytelling	Wide range of questioning techniques and skill practice activities

Training is a specialized presentation requiring complex facilitation skills that focus intensely on developing participants' skills. For example, a family friend comes to you for advice because she knows you "do presentations." She has a teenager who wants to get a driver's license. Your friend found a one-hour online presentation on how to drive a car and wants your advice. Should she have her teenager watch the presentation or send her teen to driver's education training? The answer is obvious in this stark example of the difference between presenting and training. Trainers help their audiences learn new tasks and skills, understand new processes, and comply with specialty rules or information.

What Exceptional Trainers Do Differently

When designing and delivering training, highly effective training professionals focus greater attention on three of the eight elements discussed in depth in Chapter 4: be visual, be engaging, and, most important, be brief. Let's look at each.

Be Visual

If you want to be revered for your training presentations, be highly visual. While we discuss this more in Chapter 7, here are three tips for using visuals when training professionals:

- Use models and frameworks to visually depict the steps of a process instead of five simple bullet points. Top trainers convert those into a model containing five steps. Get inspiration by searching Google Images using words like "process," "business model," or "business system."

- Eliminate all bulleted lists. (We know, this is a bulleted list, but stick with us here!) Convert bullets on a slide into graphics. If you're looking for more instruction on slide design, Mike Parkinson, author and owner of Billion Dollar Graphics (www.billiondollargraphics.com), is a master at teaching high impact designs.

- Use a little-known PowerPoint feature—the "morph" transition—to create stunning visuals and amaze participants. It's an option in the animation toolbar and can be used to create cinematic-type animations in your slides. It requires a little practice to properly set up, but it truly creates *Wow* moments for participants.

Be Engaging

This is where training is dramatically different from presenting. While you always have to engage your audience, a trainer must be capable of doing so with a variety of facilitation techniques and skill practice activities, such as our favorite—asking questions every four to six minutes. Ask these questions in a variety of forms and prompt participants to respond or separate into small groups for in-depth exercises and then regroup to compare results. That may sound difficult, but it's quite easy when you have a facilitation model to follow.

Here are some ways to engage trainees, specifically those in a virtual training session:

- Breakout rooms

- Case study reviews

- Competitions

- Polls

- Training games

- Team projects

- Whiteboards (and annotation tools)

- Participant teach-backs to the entire class

- Team projects

- Chats

By continuously encouraging engagement using different tools, training becomes highly engaging and effectively builds skills.

Be Brief

As James Clear professes in *Atomic Habits*, "Tiny changes lead to remarkable results."[1] Great trainers cut the scrap. They relentlessly discard information that does not aid the trainee. Although it may seem counterintuitive to adopt the "less is more" mindset when sharing information, it will make you incredibly successful in training presentations. Limit the information shared in your slides and participant materials to what matters and deliberately discard the rest.

One great key to being brief is to chunk it out, which means teaching a concept or task by breaking it down into parts or steps. This is often related to mind-mapping—a process to logically break down pieces of information so that action can take place. Ken Blanchard, iconic speaker and author of *The New One Minute Manager*, *One Minute Mentoring*, and *Gung Ho!*, said, "If I am concerned about having too much to say or what to cover in a speech, I organize it by mind-mapping the material."[2] Google "mind-mapping" for dozens of creative ways to organize a presentation, create reports, and more. Tony Buzan, creator and originator of mind-mapping, is a leading authority on the brain and learning techniques.[3]

The Ultimate Content Selection Checklist

While "be brief" seems simple, actually narrowing down the content to include in your training can be really difficult. As a master performance consultant, Sardék developed a system for guiding trainers through the content selection process—and it's time for you to learn that now!

Any time you are trying to decide what to include in a live in-person, virtual, or hybrid training course, use this checklist as a guide.

Include this content if the task or concept you are teaching is . . .

- Extremely important to the overall job

- Overly complex and/or hard for participants to remember

- High risk for potential errors

- A high percentage of the overall time required to complete the job

- Something that requires significant practice to meet the performance standard

- Part of a system that improves performance

- A risk to health, safety, or the environment

For content that does not satisfy any of the items in this checklist, seriously reconsider including the information in your live training. In fact, it probably should be a firm no. It can, however, be placed in an on-demand (recorded) session or simply not be included at all.

NONBUSINESS PRESENTATIONS

It was a glorious, sunny day in Yolo County, California, when Anne went skydiving for the first time. In this situation, her life depended on learning what her jumpmaster had to say.

For two days preceding her jump, Anne's jumpmaster showed her every intricacy about skydiving, including how the parachute works, what the chute looks like before it's packed, what happens if the chute doesn't open, and more. The jumpmaster left no stones unturned, repeatedly drilling Anne on the information. He emphasized safety and preparation.

The day of her jump, Anne wore her heavy parachute strapped to her back, but when it was her turn to approach the door, she couldn't get up because the weight of the pack affected her balance. She must have looked terrified, because the jumpmaster pulled her to her feet and, amid the ear-piercing wind gusts from the open aircraft door, shouted something memorable to her: "*Bruce!* You're not a hero if you do and you're not a heel if you don't!"

Eventually, she emphatically shouted back, "Good to go!" and made her way to the open door. As she got into the position as directed by the jumpmaster, Anne had little choice but to trust his instruction. When her time came to jump, she did exactly as he instructed. Exiting the aircraft, she felt the wind jerk her body and her ropes twisted. Knowing exactly how to correct the situation, Anne unwound her ropes, just as her jumpmaster taught her.

Thanks to her jumpmaster's careful life-or-death presentation, she made it to the jump zone unscathed and had the time of her life.

Anne's experience was definitely not in a business setting, and neither are many other presentations you might deliver in your daily life. You might find yourself delivering a congratulatory toast at a retirement, instructing a group of teens how to safely pitch a tent, persuading a group of friends that whitewater rafting should be your next trip, or informing your family about your new career as a presenter. You may not consider these talks a "formal" presentation because you didn't break out a slide deck, but they are nonetheless important because you have a message to deliver and your audience has a need to be met.

Although most nonbusiness presentations don't involve such high-stakes risks as skydiving, these helpful tips can make sharing your message much easier:

- **Identify with your audience.** It's great you are excited to share your message, but don't make the mistake of getting ahead of (or behind) yourself. If you go too fast, your audience might miss vital information; if you go too slow, you might sound condescending. Remember your content might be second nature to you, but it may be breaking news to your audience. Adapt your delivery to accommodate different ages in your audience (like when you're explaining something to an older or younger generation) and be sure to read the room as you go.

- **Tell, show, do (or the "teach-back" method).** For greater success presenting information, follow the formula *tell* (tell your audience what you're doing), *show* (demonstrate how or what you're doing), and *do* (let the audience take a crack at it). It's also called "teach-back." Teachers are masters of this type of presenting. The audience has a chance to practice what they've learned by teaching a lesson discovered from the presenter back to the group. Teaching others a just learned skill helps to reinforce a participant's understanding and allows new skills to sink in. And, the presenter is there to help if anyone gets stumped.

- **Give participants an opportunity to practice each part and provide feedback.** This step follows the teach-back session and could be part of an experiential exercise, where learners get to apply new techniques they've acquired to actual on-the-job needs and processes.

- **Keep it simple.** Say what you need to say simply and clearly. Don't bore your audience with unnecessary background or superfluous details, and watch out for overexplaining (that's insulting) or too much jargon (not everyone will understand).

- **Relax.** Nothing will trip you up more than your brain. So remember to breathe and relax in order to get your thoughts straight. You know what you're talking about and others are looking to you for support.

ESSENTIAL TAKEAWAYS

- Your goal in any type of presentation is to inform, instruct or educate, persuade, or entertain.

- Training requires using complex facilitation skills because of the intense focus on participant skill development.

- Training should be brief, visual, and engaging.

- Nonbusiness presentations are casual in nature and are usually delivered in a nonbusiness atmosphere.

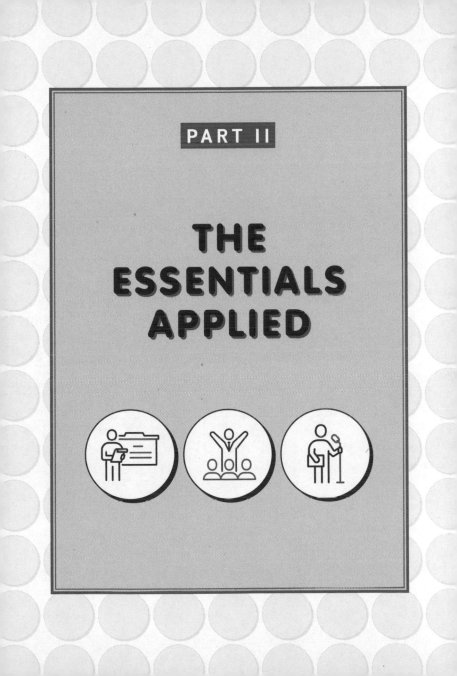

PART II

THE ESSENTIALS APPLIED

Presentation Skills Self-Assessment

This is one of our favorite sections in the book. We're big on self-evaluation, personal and professional assessments, and continuous improvement tools.

This assessment was created so you could honestly and thoughtfully evaluate your strengths and challenges thus far as a presenter. You may need some time to think through your responses. Nothing has to be completed in one sitting. We realize these statements put you in a vulnerable place and want you prepared for the accolades as well as harsh criticisms you'll undoubtedly receive along the way.

This first section of the evaluation focuses on any challenges you may face when making a presentation and examining why they are a concern for you. The purpose of this assessment is to unearth the mindsets or obstacles that may be holding you back from achieving your goals.

The second section focuses on areas you're confident in. The purpose of this part of the self-assessment is to dive deeper into the areas where you are currently excelling so you can use those to help you achieve your goals.

Directions: Please read each statement and use the following scale to indicate how strongly you agree with it. Then add up the rating column for a total score at the bottom.

    1 = Always
    2 = Usually
    3 = Sometimes
    4 = Rarely
    5 = Never

CHALLENGES	
Rating	
	My hands shake, my voice breaks, my gut lurches, or I experience other physical symptoms.
	I can't seem to gauge the body language of the group because I'm too focused on my presentation.
	I'm intimidated or afraid people won't like me.
	I have social anxiety.
	I have difficulty reading emotions in social situations.
	I feel judged by others.
	I swear too much or say the wrong thing at the wrong time.
	I get nervous in the spotlight.
	I have a stutter.
	I can't think spontaneously.
	I feel self-conscious when all eyes are on me.
	My stories don't have an end and I never know when to stop talking.
	I'm not confident in my presentation skills.
	I feel self-conscious about a disability that may or may not be noticeable to others.
	I use my flaws as an excuse not to pursue my goals.

	I'm usually unprepared and often run late.
	I have stage fright and freeze when I'm stressed.
	I get upset with myself if I'm not perfect.
	I have trouble communicating well.
	I tend to overshare.
	Maximum Score: 100

Add up your total score to determine your percentage of the 100 possible points. This score is only the "starting line"—a way to help measure your progress as you learn more about presentation applications as you keep reading. Once you've had a chance to practice your new presentation strategies, repeat this assessment to track your growth.

Right now, this benchmark assessment can also help you gain some valuable insights into your specific presentation skill levels. Any statements that you ranked as 4 or 5 may represent your strengths as a presenter. Statements that you ranked as 1, 2, or 3 provide you with opportunities for improvement.

Circle or highlight the three to five statements where you indicated the lowest scores. As you work through the next sections and begin to practice some of your presentation skills in real time, pay close attention to those areas. If you focus on improving those particular areas, you'll likely see the biggest change in your presentation performance and results.

Now it's time to understand where your confidence stands in relation to presenting. Use the scale described below and add your total score at the end.

Directions: Please read each statement and use the following scale to indicate how strongly you agree with it. Then add up the rating column for a total score at the bottom.

1 = Never
2 = Rarely
3 = Sometimes
4 = Usually
5 = Always

CONFIDENCE	
Rating	
	I am a pretty good storyteller.
	I forgive myself when I make a mistake and can move on easily.
	I am self-confident.
	I am prepared.
	I can calm my anxieties by practicing self-care.
	I'm not easily ruffled or offended.
	I can read a room and act accordingly.
	I quickly think on my feet.

	I use my strengths to my advantage and minimize my weaknesses when I can.
	My stories have a beginning, middle, and end.
	I don't hijack the spotlight.
	I practice self-forgiveness.
	I use language appropriate for the situation.
	I am fair and nonjudgmental toward others and myself.
	I stay on topic when I'm speaking.
	I take care of my physical self by regularly exercising and eating well.
	I act appropriately under pressure.
	I can take a joke.
	I am a good communicator.
	I positively influence and encourage others.
	Maximum Score: 100

Once again, add up your total score to determine your percentage of the 100 possible points. As a reminder, this score is only the "starting line." Any statements that you ranked as 4 or 5 may represent your strengths as a presenter. Statements that you ranked as 1, 2, or 3 provide you with opportunities for improvement.

As you did in the first assessment, circle or highlight the three to five statements where you indicated the lowest scores. As you work through the next sections and begin to practice some of your presentation skills in real time, pay close attention to those areas. If you focus on accelerating those particular skills, you'll likely see the biggest change in your confidence when presenting.

• • •

Becoming a credible presenter starts with self-awareness. Business and leadership legend Stephen R. Covey knew something about this subject. He said, "Self-awareness is our capacity to stand apart from ourselves and examine our thinking, our motives, our history, our scripts, our actions, and our habits and tendencies."[1] These words underscore the previous lessons in Part I. We think you'll make the cut.

CHAPTER

4

Crafting a Powerful Presentation

If you've ever watched a TED Talk, you may recognize their tagline "Ideas Worth Spreading." That's the perfect summation of a memorable presentation. Whether you're delivering a presentation to an audience of 1 or 100, you want to deliver a message the audience will find worthy of sharing with others. Presentations are a grand opportunity to influence and persuade others to your point of view. Delivering a presentation puts the spotlight on you, allowing you to stand out among your peers and develop a reputation for being a person of influence. In order to gain that title of "person of influence," a presenter must understand the makeup of a powerful presentation—and that's what this chapter focuses on.

THE MAKEUP OF A POWERFUL PRESENTATION

Every presentation has essential components. What separates an average presentation from a powerful one is arranging those components to form a memorable message. Together, let's get a basic understanding of the eight different parts that make up a powerful presentation—and we'll explore each throughout the rest of this book.

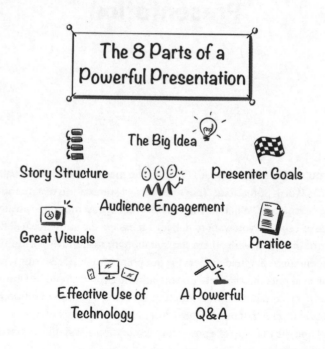

The 8 Parts of a Powerful Presentation

Story Structure

The Big Idea

Presenter Goals

Audience Engagement

Great Visuals

Pratice

Effective Use of Technology

A Powerful Q&A

1. Define the Big Idea

Have you ever listened to someone talk and found yourself asking the question, "What was the point?" That is the question every member of your audience is subconsciously asking themselves during your presentation. They want to know why they should listen, why they should care. Fail to provide compelling reasons and your presentation will fail. This places a great deal of importance on clearly defining the objective of your presentation. What is your main point? What do you want your audience to know, do, or believe as a result of listening to you? This is what we call the Big Idea Statement (review the super-simple process for developing it in Chapter 2).

2. Use Story Structure

Storytelling is the next component of a successful presentation. In her book *Resonate*, Nancy Duarte says, "Presentations are a powerfully persuasive tool, and when packaged in a story framework, your ideas become downright unstoppable."[2] Highly memorable presentations use a story structure because humans are wired to pay attention to stories.

Since the beginning of time, humans have told stories. Before the written word, stories were the main way to share information, history, and ancestry. To this day, stories help us make sense of our world, drive change, and connect with others—and we love stories because we're all storytellers. Stories provide a universal tool for communicating, inspiring, educating, and entertaining.

When building your presentation, think of it as a story being told and you stand a good chance of delivering a powerful presentation.

Chapter 5 includes a simple storytelling framework that enables you to captivate your audience with minimal effort.

3. Have Clear Presenter Goals

As a presenter, your audience expects you to deliver a great presentation. The PRESENTER acronym represents the mini-goals (in addition to your Big Idea Statement) that every speaker should strive for to deliver a captivating and memorable presentation.

PRESENTER Mini-Goals

Prepare
Rehearse
Engage
Smile
Encourage
Natural Humor
Tone and Timing
Entertain
Raise the Bar

Let's break down this acronym so you can understand the key ingredients to becoming a better presenter:

- **Prepare.** Preparation is one of your best tools to deliver a successful presentation. Arming yourself with knowledge about your subject prepares you to speak confidently, answer audience questions assertively, and present yourself as an authority in your area.

- **Rehearse.** You can't rehearse too much. Rehearse alone in front of a mirror or in front of your family, dog, cat, goldfish, or best friend. Stand up. Rehearse your gestures. Time yourself. Rehearse all the nuances of your presentation and avoid using notes whenever possible. Memorize as much as you can.

- **Engage.** To be a strong presenter, you must engage the audience. You're competing for their attention, and the only way to get and keep it is by adding value to them. Address the challenges they face. Help them see a better future. Incite them to act. Do these three things and you'll create a connection that will make you and your message memorable.

- **Smile.** Smiling makes you approachable and likeable. It also makes your message more acceptable. Presenters who smile get better results, hands down. Most presentations allow for your personality to shine through, and smiling is one of the greatest ways to convey your message and underscore your points. (However, if your presentation is serious or tragic in some way, smiling probably isn't appropriate.)

- **Encourage.** Audiences sometimes need encouragement to take action that may be difficult to start or include in their routine. Presenters can help by sharing how they introduced this action into their life and how it helped their business grow.

- **Natural humor.** Laughter is the gateway to the soul. When people laugh, they're listening. And when they are listening, you are winning as a presenter. So, whenever possible, use a little humor. Share a funny quote. Display a humorous meme—but do so without saying or doing anything that could be offensive. Using a little humor is invaluable because it makes you relatable and unforgettable.

- **Tone and timing.** Tone and timing enable you to connect with your audience on an emotional level. Within tone and timing you are creating voice tones, volume control, breathing, and pace. When you rehearse, pay attention to your voice tones, pitch, sound, and volume. How you sound and the emotions you convey make a huge difference in your message's effectiveness.

- **Entertain.** Presenting is also entertaining. That's especially true if you are presenting to adults because they expect to be entertained—unless, of course, the topic is one that entertainment would not be appropriate. The litmus test for this can be found by asking yourself after the presentation, "Will the audience say they enjoyed your presentation?" If the answer is no, review your presentation and add something the audience would find entertaining. That's where the use of appropriate humor, an intriguing image, an interesting fact or statistic, or a memorable one-liner comes into play.

- **Raise the bar.** Be better than you were the last time. If you're reading this book, we know you aspire to be the best presenter you can be and you expect to raise the bar in your next presentation. This book contains tons of fantastic tools for improving each time you present, including the Postpresentation Evaluation in the Presentation Essentials Toolkit at the end of this book. Use it to evaluate your performance after each presentation. You'll be rewarded with great audience feedback and increased opportunities to present.

4. Engage the Audience

Year after year, attendee surveys at presentations and training courses repeatedly reveal a lack of audience engagement as the top challenge presenters experience. Adults demand to be entertained, and present-ers must engage them. Here are six easy ways to instantly grab their attention, compel them to listen, and have them hanging on your every word.

Be Bold

Imagine a situation where after landing in Houston, a trainer for an oil and gas company boarded a van to get to his hotel. As the van left the airport, there was a "dinging" sound repeatedly coming from the front of the van. The trainer recognized it as the chime indicating the driver was not wearing a seatbelt. He looked at the other passengers wonder-ing if anyone would say anything. The annoying chime persisted for another three minutes. With a company requirement that all passen-gers in a moving vehicle wear a seatbelt, the trainer politely asked the driver if he was wearing his seatbelt. The driver angrily replied, "No I am not. And please don't tell me how to drive!" Not wanting to upset the driver further, the trainer politely stated his company's policy and appealed to him to wear his seatbelt for his safety and the safety of all the passengers. The driver complied and said, "You can find another ride to your hotel." He then returned to the airport.

After leaving the van, the trainer noticed all of the other passen-gers had gotten out as well. It was now past midnight, so he quickly got a taxi to his hotel. The next morning, as the trainer welcomed partici-pants to the "Courageous Leadership" course he was about to deliver, he realized several of his attendees were in the van with him the night before. *How bizarre*, he thought, because the first topic on the training agenda was the company safety policy for travel. Instead of covering the basic information contained in the first few slides, he said, "I was in a van last night with an unprofessional and unsafe driver. I knew the company policy regarding seatbelt usage: everyone has to wear a seatbelt or the vehicle cannot move. And still, I let our driver drive for over three minutes without wearing a seatbelt because I honestly was a little hesitant to say anything to the driver. Did anyone else in the van with me last night feel that way, too?" Six hands went up. The trainer then said, "Thank you for your acknowledgment. Speaking up when we see a coworker doing something unsafe is not easy, and as leaders, we are in the best position to model this behavior for our teams. It can and does protect lives."

The trainer proceeded to have a very engaging discussion using a real-world example on a sensitive topic. This was an incredibly bold move given that everyone in the class was a middle or senior manager. At the end of the discussion, something quite unexpected happened. Every individual who failed to engage the driver the night before stood up and publicly apologized to their coworkers and vowed to never let that happen again. As one leader put it, "It took courage for our trainer to do what he did last night and even more courage to do what he did just now. I am honored to have witnessed and will model his amazing display of courageous leadership from now on."

That story has been told for years inside the company and rightfully so because the trainer made a bold move. And in that moment, he made that entire presentation memorable.

Be Brief

Like most presenters, early in his career Sardék had a natural tendency to try to cover too much information in a presentation. That all changed when he worked for consulting firm Booz Allen Hamilton. He never forgot the importance of brevity he learned while there. If you had 20 slides, your senior leader would request you reduce it 2. And while it took a great deal of practice and discipline to do that, the experience he acquired was as brilliant as it was simple—include what matters (to your audience) and cut the scrap. It made his slides and presentations brief and highly focused.

Be Novel

To be novel means to be "original or striking [. . .] in conception or style."[3] The human brain ignores normal. It pays no attention to predictable. So, instead do something unexpected, striking, or original. Microsoft cofounder Bill Gates once delivered a speech about eradicating malaria from the planet. He held up a jar of mosquitoes as he explained the pests are the primary method of transmission. He then released the winged assailants into the auditorium, instantly getting the audience's attention. Don't worry! No one was infected as the mosquitoes were not carrying the malaria disease, but what Gates did was one of the most novel openers an audience will ever witness.

He knew his audience understood the key to eradicating malaria starts with attacking the source of transmission—the mosquito. He also understood the immense power of being novel from his world-changing career at Microsoft. By quickly announcing the pests were not carriers of the disease, he instantly diffused any fears, thereby guaranteeing his attention-grabbing approach would create a moment that would go viral and be talked about for decades to come.

Be Memorable

When you think of the name James Bond, you probably think of it being said as, "Bond. James Bond." Maybe you've heard the phrase, "Yeah baby yeah," said by Austin Powers. Or author James Clear's book subtitle, "Tiny Changes, Remarkable Results." Your presentation becomes very memorable by saying things that are very catchy. Share a quote . . . say a tagline . . . recite a catchphrase. Saying something worth remembering is very easy when you have a method you can follow. We'll share several techniques for creating memorable statements in Chapter 8.

Be Confident

We've all seen a person who exudes confidence. What does that really mean for a presenter? How can we show that we are confident? Well, knowing your content is the first place to start. Practice delivering your presentation so that you can deliver it even if the electricity goes out in the entire town causing you to deliver it outside with no tech involved (that actually happened to one of the authors). Speak clearly by articulating your words and projecting your voice. Stand with your back straight. And smile when appropriate. Do these simple things and you'll come across as a confident presenter.

Be Adaptable

The Covid-19 pandemic unleashed a seismic transformation in the way presentations are delivered. Presenters are now expected to be fully capable of delivering presentations in person as well as virtually across multiple platforms. That's an extreme example of being adaptable.

Adaptability is more about being able to change course without losing focus or the ability to function. Being adaptable means having backup resources if you need them, such as a copy of your presentation on a flash drive. It also means knowing what to do if participant materials don't show up or participants experience technical issues when attending your virtual presentation. Whom can you contact for help when these things inevitably happen? And finally, if your client cuts the time allotted for your presentation, you've got to be capable of adapting on the fly without missing a beat. The more you're prepared, the more adaptable you'll be.

For your next presentation, use these tips as a quick reference checklist. It will help you avoid drowning your audience in data. It will keep you focused on their needs. And it will give you a reasonable chance at crafting a powerful presentation, one that is memorable and impactful.

6 Keys to Audience Engagement

Be Bold

Be Brief

Be Novel

Be Memorable

Be Confident

Be Adaptable

5. Use Great Visuals

If you want to deliver a memorable presentation, take to heart what is widely known in Hollywood: show business is a show and a business. This also applies to your presentation. The "show" component of a presentation requires the speaker to paint a picture for the audience. That often includes using images in a PowerPoint deck or other presentation software. There are many online sources and tools containing images to fit your presentation topic, and we share our favorites in Chapter 7.

Experienced presenters also use descriptive language, metaphors, and analogies to create a picture in the audience's mind. For example, "The stakes are gigantic. Low priced competitors are ripping our profitability to shreds. Getting moms to buy our infant clothing line in a postpandemic world requires us to burrow our way through the clutter in a society that lives online with too many choices and too little attention to care about anything other than price."

If you want to be memorable, use descriptive language to say something worth remembering. We show you how to craft memorable catchphrases and one-liners in Chapter 8.

6. Be Proficient with the Technology

Prior to the pandemic, the majority of presentations were delivered in person, but that has shifted drastically. Now presenters are expected to be able to deliver presentations in person, online, and a hybrid of both. Because of this, it's crucial you understand and can effectively use the technology required for each and every one of your presentations. In Chapter 10 we'll explore this topic and review the technology required to deliver content online.

7. Practice

Practice! Practice! Practice! Former professional basketball player Bill Bradley once said, "When you're not practicing, someone somewhere is. And when the two of you meet, given roughly equal ability, he will win."[4] To use a sports analogy, play like you're in first. Train like you're in second. To deliver an effective presentation, follow this simple, three-step plan:

- **Rehearse.** This may seem obvious; however, we know from coaching thousands of presenters there is a tendency to invest too little time and effort in rehearsing. Rehearsing enables you to not only embed the content of your presentation in your mind, it also develops the muscle memory to ensure your body language is in synch with your message delivery. Don't practice your presentation until you can get it right; practice your presentation until you can't get it wrong.

- **Get feedback.** Blooper videos from movies and TV shows are entertaining to watch and serve an insanely valuable purpose. They provide amazing feedback to the actors. Recording yourself as you rehearse does the exact same thing for you. Alternatively, ask a friend, family member, or colleague to observe your rehearsal and provide feedback. Evaluated rehearsal separates the mediocre presenters from the exceptional presenters. Be the exception.

- **Use visualization.** You've probably heard athletes describe how they envisioned taking the last shot to win the game before they actually did it. Visualization is a potent weapon in the presenter's toolkit because it predicts a future you create by practicing your way into it. Visit where you will deliver your presentation to get a feel for the room. Walk through the space, visualizing things from the audience's perspective so you can sense what their experience will be like when you present. If you're delivering the presentation virtually, schedule time with the event planner to conduct a dry run in the virtual platform. And imagine how great it's going to feel to nail that presentation!

We've had the pleasure of mentoring Rusty Shields, CEO of Develefy Consulting, who has excelled at using these three preparation steps. His transformation has been nothing short of astounding. He went from a soft-spoken and likeable individual to a powerful presenter who projects confidence whenever he is before an audience. Recently, he was accepted by the Association for Talent Development (ATD) to become a member of their elite faculty who deliver ATD courses. When asked what he attributes his success as a trainer to, he cited his unwavering dedication to preparation as the difference maker. He's a shining example of a simple truth—the more effort you invest in preparing for success as a presenter, the greater the success you'll experience.

8. Nail the Answers in Your Q&A

You've delivered an amazing presentation. The audience was engaged, and your message resonated. Now it's time for the question-and-answer (Q&A) session. Interestingly enough, very few presentation skills courses cover this critical presentation component, so we're going to share a few tips to help you become proficient at handling it.

Tasha Jones is the perfect example of someone who has learned to own the room during a Q&A session. As a vice president for Eggleston, a rehabilitation services provider in southeastern Virginia, she gives frequent presentations to executives inside her company and to regulatory and compliance officials who oversee service providers in her industry. The information she shares can be very technical, and she has a natural preference to go into great detail when sharing information and answering questions.

She wanted to enhance her executive presence and presentations skills, and one area we focused on with her was reducing the amount of detail she shared during presentations and Q&A sessions. During our coaching sessions, we discovered she loves cheerleading so much that she coaches youngsters as a hobby. So, we knew she possessed a deep understanding of the power of "sticking the landing" during a performance. Using her background as a cheerleading coach, we coached her using what we call the posture, vocal variety, and succinct (PVS) model. Once she stood up straight, varied her speaking patterns, and kept her answers short, sweet, and to the point, her confidence skyrocketed, and the results were profound. Her staff was thrilled with the reduction in the level of detail she provided, and she received accolades from her CEO and others regarding her presentations.

She is a rising star as both a leader and a presenter, and we antici pate seeing her on some very big stages as more organizations become aware of her thought leadership and powerful presentation skills.

Follow the PVS model, and you will project confidence, speak with charisma, and deliver a strong close to your presentation.

WHAT LASTING IMPRESSION WILL YOU MAKE AS A PRESENTER?

In closing, we share this thought with you. The phrase "you never get a second chance to make a first impression" hits home with a lot of presenters. It takes less than three seconds for someone to form an opinion of you based on the first impression. Keep this in mind as you continue through the remaining chapters.

Armed with these essential elements of a powerful presentation, you're well on your way to creating a lasting impression and influencing each and every person who has the opportunity to receive the gift of your knowledge and expertise via your presentation.

ESSENTIAL TAKEAWAYS

- Great presentations begin with the Big Idea Statement.
- Stories captivate audiences and keep them engaged.
- The PRESENTER acronym contains mini-goals every presenter should strive for: *P*repare, *R*ehearse, *E*ngage, *S*mile, *E*ncourage, *N*atural humor, *T*one and timing, *E*ntertain, and *R*aise the bar.
- If you're not engaging your audience, you risk losing their attention.
- Successful presenters use great visuals, descriptive language, metaphors, and analogies to create pictures in their audiences' minds.
- Familiarize yourself with the latest presentation technology.

The Power of Storytelling

If the purpose of a presentation is to persuade, storytelling is the most powerful tool for achieving that goal. Through storytelling, you invite members of the audience into your experience and give them the ultimate opportunity to visualize things from your point of view.

A presentation that uses story structure as its foundation can be incredibly irresistible and highly seductive to an audience because, as author Tamsen Webster says, "You need to build a story that people will tell themselves about your idea" and "your idea becomes theirs."[1] Stories work because they're what we naturally use to make sense of the world. If storytelling is so powerful and continues to be one of the most popular skills to develop in the world of business, why do most presenters fail to tell good stories during their presentations? Let's explore that together.

EVERYONE TELLS STORIES— FEW PERSUADE

Herein lies a massive problem: everyone tells stories, but few of those stories persuade. You've probably been the victim of someone rambling on and on, spewing a torrent of irrelevant, useless information. Or maybe the speaker forgot what he or she was saying and began repeating what was already said or, worse yet, started telling another unrelated story. Perhaps you've been that speaker who created this "monologue with hostages" experience yourself.

Few of those stories persuade, and if you're selling a product, trying to get a raise, attempting to convince a donor to give you a large sum of money, or even instructing a colleague on how to properly fill out a form—that's going to be a big problem. A storyteller must always keep the audience in mind when telling a story: *What does my audience need to know, or what problem does my audience have that my story will address?* How you persuade your audience depends on how convincingly you can respond to what the problem or challenge is.

We see this too often during presentations—the presenter neglects to fulfill the audience's needs. How often have you sat through a presentation containing slides bursting at the seams with so much information you stopped paying attention, quietly begging for a merciful end to your misery? Or maybe you've listened to a fun story but wondered what the actual point was. If our stories are fun to listen to but fail to get to the point (by answering the "What's in it for the audience?" question), why should our audience listen?

A successful presenter follows a proven structure for persuading listeners. This chapter shares a storytelling formula to ensure you capture your audience's attention during your presentation, tapping into their imaginations and taking them on a journey.

CRAFTING STORIES THAT ARE SIMPLY IRRESISTIBLE

Your favorite movies, books, or TV shows follow a story structure. At its core, a persuasive story leads a listener to change perspective because people must change their perspective before they are willing to take action to change. A powerful persuasive story uses reason and logic to paint a picture that the presenter's idea is valid and superior. The speaker uses facts, sound reasoning, and evidence to support his or her argument. That's why the Big Idea Statement—a creative way of simplifying your main point into an easily understandable and convincing position—is so incredibly effective and reliable. It gets right to the point, keeping your audience's attention.

There are numerous storytelling frameworks available that contain common elements on effective storytelling. These frameworks range from the simple to the extraordinarily complex. However, all storytelling frameworks contain a few basic elements.

Think of your favorite movie. It follows a predictable and proven process. The movie starts with the main character (the Hero). The Hero encounters a problem that ultimately leads to a life-altering decision (the Moment of Truth). The Hero takes action and ultimately achieves the goal (saves the day, wins the game, solves the crime, etc.). This is commonly known as the Hero's Journey. An effective presentation uses the Hero's Journey to take listeners on a transformational journey from "what is" to "what can be." In our experience as professional speakers and authors, we've found a simple, easy, and effective approach to use in persuasive presentations: the High-Impact Storytelling Formula. This is a "plug-and-play" formula for building your own irresistibly transformational journey into your presentations.

The High-Impact Storytelling Formula

Every story contains three characters:

With those basic characters, we can now use the High-Impact Storytelling Formula to construct a highly persuasive presentation because we know people must change their perspective before they will take action on our messages.

Step 1: Identify the Hero. Define your main character and answer the question: "What does the Hero want?" In a presentation, your client/audience is the Hero.

Step 2: Define the Villain. The Villain is the second of the three characters in a story and it represents the problem, challenge, or barrier preventing the Hero from getting what he or she wants.

Step 3: Expose the Conflict. How does the existence of the Villain make the Hero feel? That's the conflict. The conflict can also be between what the Hero wants and what the Hero believes to be true. The level of conflict the Hero experiences should increase as your story unfolds.

Step 4: Define the Moment of Truth. In *Find Your Red Thread*, Tamsen Webster defines the moment of truth as "something that creates an internal conflict in the minds of your audience."[2] It creates a point of no return for the Hero and makes inaction impossible. The Hero must act in order to have any chance of achieving the goal.

Step 5: Introduce the Guide. The Guide, the third character in a story, provides the advice, support, or solution required for the Hero to achieve the goal. In your presentation, you (or the solution) serve as the Guide.

Step 6: Take Action. The Hero uses the solution. In your presentation, this is a great place to share an example of a client using your solution to achieve the goal.

By crafting presentations using story structure, you:

- Eliminate irrelevant information
- Obliterate confusion
- Engage your audience
- Inspire action

The High-Impact Storytelling Formula

Step 1: Identify the Hero

Step 2: Define the Villain

Step 3: Expose the Conflict

Step 4: Define the Moment of Truth

Step 5: Introduce the Guide

Step 6: Take Action

Whether you are a vice president of sales, operations manager, small business owner, or nonprofit employee, using the High-Impact Storytelling Formula will transform the way you think, how you communicate, and the results you achieve with your presentations.

Let's look at an example to see exactly how this formula plays out in real life.

Example: Improve Employee Engagement in a Healthcare Provider

A healthcare organization composed of several hospitals, clinics, and physician offices was experiencing unprecedented levels of voluntary turnover of critical staff. The CEO decided to host a leadership summit for the top 300 leaders to address the impact of turnover on the organization's ability to safely serve the people of its communities.

Step 1: Identify the Hero

In this scenario, the Hero is every manager in the organization.

Step 2: Define the Villain

The problem to be addressed was high voluntary turnover, but turnover was high in three critical job roles. The CEO picked only one role to address in the leadership summit: voluntary turnover in the nursing staff. With that decision made, the question to be answered was: What is causing nurses to voluntarily leave the organization? Through exit interviews and a review of leading healthcare industry publications, three main drivers of nurse turnover were identified:

- Insufficient staffing levels

- Significant increased competition for nurses due to industry demand outstripping supply

- Nurses feeling overworked and not supported by their immediate managers, who were similarly lacking support from their senior managers

After hearing this information from the vice president of Human Resources, the CEO and executive leadership team decided voluntary turnover was the Villain to defeat.

Step 3: Expose the Conflict

The Heroes (managers) are struggling to keep up morale for themselves and their teams because the demands for services far outstrip their capacity to meet the needs. As the employees' struggle to survive each shift increases, managers fail to provide positive reinforcement and appreciation to their staff. Workers complain about being overworked, creating a vicious cycle of blame and reblame for a lack of quality and safety in patient care.

As the challenges of being understaffed increase, this further exposes the conflict managers are experiencing and they become more demanding, less flexible, and less available for addressing problems. Nurses, who are on the front lines of patient care, are caught in the middle of what often becomes a hostile working environment. In a few high-profile national cases, mistakes made by exhausted nurses in other healthcare providers led to patient deaths, leading to calls for politicians to further regulate the healthcare industry to address the unsafe working conditions.

Step 4: Define the Moment of Truth

The Moment of Truth is when the Hero must take action to achieve a desired goal. In this case, nurses were voluntarily leaving the organization, creating a significant staffing shortage endangering patient care. Managers were in dire need to hire replacement nursing staff as soon as possible. Their only option was to hire nurses participating in the travel nursing program, a national effort created to address the unprecedented increase in the demand for nurses and the lack of staffing due to the pandemic. The travel nurse program offered nurses an opportunity to go on contract with hospitals and earn up to three to five times more than their typical pay per shift.

As a result, the nurse staffing shortage became the Moment of Truth as the staffing shortage forced management to take action to offset the hemorrhaging of nurses.

Step 5: Introduce the Guide

Now it's time for the CEO (the Guide) to present how the new plan will be put into action. The Guide's role in this presentation is to provide the advice, support, or solution to the Hero—in this case the 300 managers attending the summit. With the Villain defined as voluntary turnover, the CEO decided to lead the effort of transformation and equip his management team with the skills and tools needed to improve manager/employee relations. He put together a team of senior leaders and hired an outside leadership expert to coach and train the entire leadership team.

As a sidenote, in most cases, when delivering a presentation, you are the Guide because you're going to offer a solution to a problem the audience is experiencing. It's worth noting the Guide can be anyone who can effectively serve in the role, whether it be an internal resource such as an employee or an external resource such as a consultant or speaker.

Step 6: Take Action

After the leadership summit, all managers (the Heroes) were given an action plan to adopt the strategies learned during the summit. HR launched a comprehensive implementation plan that included weekly follow-ups to ensure managers were actively completing their action plans. To the CEO's delight, two months after the summit, the VP of HR reported a reduction in nurse voluntary turnover and an increase in customer satisfaction scores.

• • •

As you can see, you can take any given scenario and plug it into the formula to construct a story. But now you might be wondering how this formula actually gets transformed into a story. So it's time to show you how that's done.

In the next section, we'll continue with the story we just worked through, highlighting each step from the formula so you can see how the story was constructed. Then we'll take you through the steps to create your own high-impact stories.

The Story of Improving Employee Engagement in a Healthcare Provider

Managers in a large hospital chain struggled mightily in the midst of the Covid-19 pandemic (Hero: the managers). The hospitals were overrun with Covid patients, and the medical teams were experiencing severe burnout. To compound matters, the most critical role at ground zero of patient care was the nurse, and the hospitals were losing them to the competition by the dozens on a monthly basis (Villain: voluntary turnover). This was keeping the CEO up at night and had his full attention (Guide: the CEO), so he directed his VP of HR to identify why nurses were leaving. The results of the report were shocking. The VP of HR explained the main reason nurses were quitting was not due to better pay, which is what everyone assumed was the main reason. Nurses were leaving because they were overworked due to understaffing and had opportunities to go to competitors (conflict: understaffing leading to excessive workloads).

The VP of HR presented this information to the CEO and executive leadership team, explaining that managers would often require nurses to work double and triple shifts without breaks. In addition, there was a lack of proper equipment and supplies due to persistent supply chain issues. Patient and employee care and safety were the CEO's top priorities, and with voluntary turnover endangering patient care, he decided he had to get his leaders some help (Moment of Truth: high nurse turnover endangering patient care). He directed the VP of HR to schedule a summit for the top 300 leaders during which a select team of internal leaders and an external leadership expert would provide training on the tools required to improve the manager/employee relationship and address the supply issues.

At the summit, the keynote speaker opened with a story describing how a simple mistake at another hospital made by a nurse led to the tragic death of a patient. At the end of the story, the speaker revealed the patient who died was his father. No one in the audience, including the CEO, knew this about the keynote speaker. As he closed his presentation, the speaker painted a picture of a better future, one in which the hospital chain not only retains its nurses but attracts qualified talent from the travel nursing program and other sources to become the healthcare provider of choice in the region.

There was a renewed sense of dedication and purpose among those in the room after this story was told and the presentation ended.

The CEO closed the meeting and invited every leader to own the transformation to better relationships and improved employee engagement. With support from the CEO and an HR implementation plan, managers focused on improving relationships with their direct reports (Hero takes action: managers complete their action plans). Two months after the summit, to the CEO's delight, the VP of HR reported nurse voluntary turnover had dropped and customer satisfaction scores had improved.

• • •

With this example story behind us, let's recap the story structure process one last time.

Your story starts with the main character (known as the Hero). In business presentations, tell at least one story where the audience (or a past client) was the Hero. And, as enticing as it may be, limit the number of stories you tell where you are the Hero because telling too many stories about you can make you appear to be focused on your accomplishments and interest.

Once the Hero is identified, you need to define the problem the Hero encounters (known as the Villain).

From there, you share that the Villain causes conflict. The situation keeps getting worse, thereby increasing the level of challenge the Hero is experiencing, which is known as exposing the conflict.

The conflict reaches a climax (known as the Moment of Truth) forcing the Hero to seek advice or a solution from another character in the story (known as the Guide).

Finally, the Hero takes action using the Guide's advice or solution, and as a result of taking action, the Hero achieves the goal (solves the problem, makes a positive change, etc.). An effective presentation uses the Hero's Journey to take the audience on a transformation journey from "what is" to "what can be."

Additional Tips and Strategies for Telling Stories

While using the High-Impact Storytelling Formula to construct and tell stories is incredibly effective, here are a few additional tips so you can become the best storyteller you can be:

Keep stories short. Stories told in a business presentation should generally be two minutes or less. That may sound very challenging to do, but look at any professional speaker and you'll see their stories are delivered in less than two minutes. This requires eliminating unnecessary information. Stories longer than two minutes risk losing audience interest, and we generally advise against longer stories until you're a seasoned storyteller. Use the High-Impact Storytelling Formula to cut the fat from your story until you hit the target length.

Use descriptive language. Make use of analogies, metaphors, and memorable catchphrases in your stories to paint a picture in the minds of your audience. (You'll learn more about memorable catchphrases and one-liners in Chapter 8.)

Use "power" words as well. Power words evoke an emotion—words like "boost," "surprising," "reduced," and "uncover." These words are particularly effective when used in your call to action. Here is an example of a call to action with the power words underlined. In summary, a speaker might say, "Take control of your destiny. By using the ABC solution, you will shorten the time to sale and dominate the market." To find more such words, simply Google "power words" and you'll find several lists to choose from.

Rehearse to sound conversational. Stories need to sound conversational, not scripted. This requires dedicated time practicing. We know it's an obvious tip, but the difference between sounding scripted and conversational can make or break your effectiveness as a speaker.

Use sources to find great stories. You may be wondering where to find stories. While it will depend on the problem you are addressing in your presentation, there are generally 10 great sources of stories:

- **Your personal experience.** You are a wealth of information and experience. Use it.

- **Your organization's sales, operations, and customer service staff.** They are in direct contact with customers and will have amazing stories to share with you.

- **TED Talks, podcasts, and blogs.** These serve as credibility-boosting sources because they are usually published by domain experts.

- **Professional speakers.** Another excellent source of stories. Like all professional speakers, we tell stories in our presentations. Sardék shares stories of his experiences while traveling to and working with clients in 32 countries. Those include stories of being lost in the Libyan desert with a client, helping leaders working in war-torn regions form deep and meaningful relationships with employees, training sales teams how to deliver highly engaging presentations, and more. Anne talks about TV and movie industry mishaps, and on-the-campaign-trail, political stomping ground presentations. The entertainment industry and political arenas depend on great presentations and storytelling—it's what sustains them.

- **TV shows.** Documentaries can be excellent sources of stories, and channels like Discovery and the History Channel are full of great material.

- **Customers.** An obvious source, stories of helping customers always serve you well.

- **Books, magazines, newspapers, and more.** All of these are great sources of stories.

- **Social media platforms.** Approach with extreme caution. With the rise in disinformation, you have be careful with information found in social media. Check your sources and verify your information!

- **Industry trends.** Industry associations, unions, and research organizations are full of stories.

- **History.** Historical archives, museums, and biographies are excellent sources of stories.

• • •

Armed with the High-Impact Storytelling Formula and additional tips (including keep your stories short, use descriptive language, and rehearse to sound conversational), you can easily craft and tell stories that captivate an audience and make your message memorable.

ESSENTIAL TAKEAWAYS

- Storytelling is a powerful tool for persuasion.
- Storytellers should always keep their audience in mind.
- Follow the storytelling framework of the Hero's Journey to take your audience from "what is" to "what can be."
- The Hero's Journey follows a six-step process: identify the Hero (audience), define the Villain (the problem), expose the Conflict, define the Moment of Truth, introduce the Guide (gives the solution), and (the Hero) takes action.

CHAPTER

6

13 Attention-Grabbing Openers

The opening of your presentation is critically important—it is the very first time you are asking for your audience's attention. Presentation openers serve several purposes. They are the gateway to the mind of your audience, enabling you to grab their attention, pique their interest, and establish a connection. Openers also evoke an emotion in the members of your audience, one you can repeatedly refer to as you take them on the journey to a better future. Openers are great for asking provocative questions that cause your audience to think—to consider your Big Idea. Asking "what if" is a classic opener used by many TEDx speakers. Finally, openers enable you to demonstrate vulnerability. Bestselling author, researcher, and popular keynote speaker Brené Brown has built her entire brand around being vulnerable because it makes a person human. Think of your presentation opener like this: If your goal is to reach the moon, your opener is the first stage of the rocket that will take you there. In this chapter are 13 proven ways to begin a presentation with a bang. We encourage you to bookmark it as it is a great reference guide for crafting an attention-grabbing opening.

1. TELL A STORY

You already know much about storytelling from previous chapters, but it still needs to be included as number one on this list because that's how important it is. Stories are the portal to the human imagination, and starting your presentation with a story is a failproof way to instantly own the room.

2. USE HUMOR

At the top of his 2016 TED Talk, speaker Ken Robinson cracked a joke. He went on to garner three laughs from the audience in just 30 seconds. While that may not be unusual, he averaged an astonishing two laughs per minute over his entire speech (which approaches humor royalty numbers of the movie *The Hangover* at 2.5 laughs per minute). His TED Talk has been viewed more than 73 million times, making it the most watched TED Talk of all time. And he did that with a speech titled "Do Schools Kill Creativity?"[1] Hardly a subject that evokes images of a crowd laughing repeatedly.

Humor works so well because it initiates biological warfare as it triggers the release of dopamine to our brains. And the good news is you don't have to be funny to put humor into your presentation. Often, all it takes is sharing an experience that made you laugh. As sales coach Jeffrey Gitomer says, "The end of laughter is followed by the height of listening."[2] Get them laughing, and you've got them actively listening.

It is important to ensure the humor is appropriate, so use it with caution, and if in doubt, leave it out.

Humor works so well because it triggers the release of dopamine to our brains.

3. PROVIDE A STATISTIC

Powerful statistics can make an impact on an audience.

- A drunk driver will, on average, drive drunk 80 times before being arrested for the first time. This is an attention-grabbing statistic from Mothers Against Drunk Driving (MADD).[3]

- A one terabyte thumb drive can hold 200,000 songs.

- During the Great Resignation of 2021, 40 percent of employees said they were considering leaving their job in the next three to six months.[4]

- Leigh Branham, author of *The 7 Hidden Reasons Employees Leave*,[5] revealed that 89 percent of bosses believe employees quit because they want more money, but the reality is only 12 percent of employees leave an organization for more money.

- Multiple surveys of managers conducted over several years have consistently revealed roughly 60 percent of all managers have never received management training.

After reading these statistics, you're likely experiencing the same emotions and reactions that an audience would experience—shock and wow. We love using statistics in the beginning of a presentation because they create an element of surprise while also bringing in facts to back up your ideas. They also are an excellent tool for painting a picture to support the key message of your presentation. So, conduct a little research to find the perfect attention-grabber for your presentation.

4. SHARE A QUOTE

Quotes can create those golden "aha" moments that audiences love. It's perfectly fine to use quotes written by others, as long as you give them credit.

You elevate your game to a new level when you create your own quotes. Here are some examples we've written:

- "You cannot manage people, so focus on managing relationships." —Anne Bruce

- "Growth and convenience never coexist." —Sardék Love

Using your own quotes is such a powerful tool in the presenter's toolkit that we teach a few simple techniques for writing memorable catchphrases and one-liners in Chapter 8.

5. SHOW A VIDEO

Coinciding with the explosive growth in smartphone usage, video has become a favorite tool for presenters of all skill levels. Social media platforms boast the addition of millions of new videos daily—and for good reason. Videos instantly grab the audience's attention, enabling the presenter to communicate a message in an engaging manner. Videos also serve as a fantastic launch point for discussions that will happen after the presentation. Finally, videos break the monotony by adding variety to a presentation. With editing capabilities at your fingertips, you can shoot, edit, and publish custom videos from your smartphone that tap directly into the hearts and minds of your audience.

6. ASK A QUESTION

Marilee Adams, author of *Change Your Questions, Change Your Life,*[6] says great results begin with great questions because thinking actually occurs as an internal question-and-answer process. We agree. Asking a provocative question related to your message creates tension for the audience, which is critical because there must be tension for your message to grab their attention. According to comedian Zahra Noorbakhsh, tension sets up the desire to see a problem—however big or small—get resolved.[7]

So, you might be wondering what questions to ask as a presentation opener. Think of opening questions as buttons that, when pressed, evoke an emotion in our audience. Depending on the list you use, there are seven basic human emotions. When crafting an opening question, we search for questions that could evoke the emotion that fits our message.

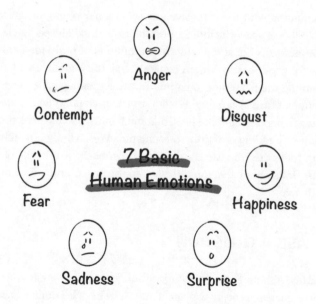

Novice presenters should concentrate on using questions that evoke happiness or (a good or pleasant) surprise. It takes a bit of skill to use the remaining five emotions, so we recommend these only to more advanced and experienced speakers.

Once you have the emotion you wish to induce, it's just a matter of brainstorming questions that evoke them based on your topic or message. Here are some examples, starting with evoking a pleasant surprise.

Think about your product, service, organization, or overall topic. What would people find pleasantly surprising about any of those? If your topic is to motivate your audience to not view failure as a barrier to massive success, you could ask this question: "How many times are you willing to fail if you were guaranteed success in the future?" Then you could share the story that Walt Disney was fired from a Missouri newspaper for not being creative enough.

Here's another example. If you speak to leaders, ask them the ultimate leadership question, "Do you make other people's lives more complex or more complete?"

Take the time to brainstorm a list of questions until one stands out as a good fit for your opener. Usually, you'll find a great question if you brainstorm a list of 5 to 10 questions. That's the process. It's simple and repeatable, and it reveals an impactful question. If you want your audience to buy into you and your message, start by provoking them with a question.

7. USE ACTIVITIES AND ICEBREAKERS

Gone are the days of speakers burying audiences in heaps of data and information. With a large percentage of presentations being delivered virtually in a postpandemic world, the battle for audience attention is fierce. Engaging audiences with interaction is now the norm, and it is relatively easy to do when using activities and icebreakers. The key is selecting an activity or an icebreaker that meets these criteria:

- **It is feasible to use based on the size of your audience.**
  Unless you are an experienced speaker, activities that require
  materials or props should be limited to smaller audiences.
  Otherwise you run the risk of experiencing a wide variety of
  potential problems doing the activity.

- **It is relevant to your topic.** Be sure to explicitly link the
  activity or icebreaker to your topic so that your audience
  clearly understands the connection between the two.

- **It can be done quickly.** If used at the beginning of a
  presentation, the activity should be completed in five minutes
  or less to avoid becoming an unintended distraction from
  your main point.

Here is a very popular memory activity to get your audience immediately engaged.

Activity: Memory Test

Description: People assume they are very good at
remembering things. This is a fascinating and fun activity
that exposes our inability to remember much of what we hear
and see.

Materials Required: Each person needs a pen or pencil and
single sheet of paper. Alternatively, each attendee can type
answers in the notes on their personal devices.

The presenter needs to create a slide listing 16 words.
Be sure the audience has the materials before beginning the
activity.

Time Required: 5 minutes

Speaker Setup: Prepare a slide deck.

Slide 1 should contain these instructions: *Listen to the list of words as I share them.*

Each remaining slide should contain the single word as shown in this list:

Slide 2: Dream

Slide 3: Sleep

Slide 4: Night

Slide 5: Snooze

Slide 6: Sheet

Slide 7: Nod

Slide 8: Tired

Slide 9: Night

Slide 10: Insomnia

Slide 11: Artichoke

Slide 12: Blanket

Slide 13: Night

Slide 14: Alarm

Slide 15: Snore

Slide 16: Pillow

Slide 17: *Write down as many words as you can remember.*

Instructions for the Audience:

Running the Activity:

- Show your first slide to the audience and explain the instructions.

- Display each word for two seconds while reading it aloud to the audience before moving to the next word.

- Once the list is complete, read the instructions on slide 17 aloud.

- Then tell the audience they have one minute to write down as many words as they can remember and say, "Go!" Set a timer running for one minute.

Debrief the Activity:

Once the minute is up, ask:

> How many words did you write down? (Get a few responses from your audience. Typically, the numbers written down will range from 4 to 11.)

This activity is a great way to prove we don't retain information as well as we think, which can then be a setup to address the many challenges that arise in business. As a reminder, explicitly link the activity to a key point in your presentation.

If you would like additional high-impact activities to use in your presentations, go to https://sardeklove.com to get free access to several to instantly engage your audience.

8. DO A DEMONSTRATION

Due to the pandemic, it was the first time the company's top leaders had assembled in person in three years. The theme of their leadership conference was "Make Magic," and they were meeting at the Disney

Yacht Club in Florida. In his opening, the CEO said, "We have to build a wall of customer delight, and to do that requires us to actively inspect every brick every day." He said this while placing bricks on top of bricks. The point of his demonstration was that the magic in their company is not in the brick, it's in the delight they create by actively inspecting their bricks every day to ensure each brick is aligned. Through that alignment, they can consistently deliver the delight their customers deserve and expect. That small wall of customer delight became the focal point for his message and the entire leadership conference.

Demonstrations are great for creating buzz and often become the most memorable moments in a presentation. You can do a product demonstration or bring a volunteer onstage or to the front of the room to participate in some form of a demonstration. The options are only limited by your creativity. Demonstrations can be an ingenious strategy to open a presentation with a bang, so unleash your creativity and you'll uncover innovative ways to inspire, excite, and intrigue your audience.

9. SHARE A MEME OR IMAGE

People naturally think in images. It's how we see the world, and the pictures we hold in our mind determine how we feel. Savvy marketers know this all too well, and they bombard us with images designed to evoke a feeling because action always follows feelings. Use this to your advantage.

When teaching speakers how to select a meme or image to evoke an emotion in their audience, we have them use the pictures/emotions/actions (PEA) framework. It works like this. In order to identify the right *picture* to use, identify the *actions* you want the audience to take and then ask yourself what *emotions* cause people to take those desired actions? Make a list of those emotions and find images that evoke each emotion. By following the PEA framework, you'll find images that grab your audience's attention.

10. ATTACK OR CHALLENGE THE STATUS QUO

In most presentations, the goal is to get the audience to change. This is the crux of the Big Idea. Attacking the status quo or the norm is a pro-vocative technique sure to garner audience attention.

Think of your presentation as having one of the following goals—to convince the audience to:

- Stop what they are doing.

- Start doing something new.

With one of those goals in mind, it's relatively simple to identify an attention-grabbing opener that sets the stage for taking the audience on a inspiring journey to consider taking the action you want them to take.

For example, one manager we coached wanted to impress upon her staff the importance of using strong passwords when working re-motely. She discovered the most commonly used password (123456) is an open invitation for hackers as it is easily exploited to access data.[8] Because of this, she reached out to several direct reports to determine if they used the hackers' favorite exploitable password. To her dismay, nearly 40 percent of those surveyed admitted they used it. Armed with this evidence and a little coaching from us on how to open her presentation with a bang, she begins her presentation by displaying a slide with that password taking up the entire frame.

That is a masterful example of inciting the audience to stop doing something they are doing and take immediate action.

Think of the norms in your organization that you're trying to create or change. Brainstorm a list and based on your presentation's Big Idea Statement, pick a situation that would be the perfect scenario for encouraging your listeners to stop or to start doing something specific. Do so, and you'll immediately grab their attention.

11. PLAY AN AUDIO CLIP

Audio clips allow you to create an experience and instantly transport your listeners inside the experience. This can be anything from podcast clips, customer testimonials, comments from leaders, or employee messages. All are great sources of audio clips; use them whenever possible.

12. CONDUCT A POLL OR SURVEY

With the exponential growth in virtual presentations, polling and surveying audiences during a live presentation has become easy and inexpensive. Savvy presenters can use the results from live surveys and polls later in their presentations, making them super engaging. This is a commonly used tool during a live presentation because it is a viable and important option for grabbing attention fast.

13. MAKE A BOLD CLAIM

"We choose to go to the moon. We choose to go to the moon in this decade and do the other things, not because they are easy, but because they are hard, because that goal will serve to organize and measure the best of our energies and skills, because that challenge is one that we are willing to accept, one we are unwilling to postpone, and one which we intend to win."[9] This bold claim of winning the race to be the first country to land on the moon was made by President John F. Kennedy in his 1962 speech at Rice University in Houston. You can do the same. Take a stand. Be bold. It can be a tremendous launching pad for you to inspire change and transformation. Unlike the popular phrase—the meek will most likely *not* inherit the Earth.

• • •

By using any of these 13 methods to open a presentation, you avoid the trap of being predictable. Predictability breeds boredom and disengagement. Be novel. Be different. It's not hard. It just requires intention and confidence.

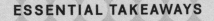

ESSENTIAL TAKEAWAYS

- Strong openers help you hook your audience immediately.
- Use any of these 13 ways to open your presentation to start strong:

    1. Tell a story
    2. Use humor
    3. Provide a statistic
    4. Share a quote
    5. Show a video
    6. Ask a question
    7. Use activities and icebreakers
    8. Do a demonstration
    9. Share a meme or image
    10. Attack or challenge the status quo
    11. Play an audio clip
    12. Conduct a poll or survey
    13. Make a bold claim

Presenting Visually
Stunning Images

The host of the online meeting turned the presentation over to John. John said a few pleasantries and then shared his screen for all to see. Immediately, attendees began to check out, multitask, or log off entirely. Oblivious to the impact his first slide was having, John launched into a monotone reading of all 15 bulleted items he had carefully curated to share.

At bullet number nine, the host interrupted John and asked, "Hey John, since we have this list in the handout you provided, which of these items are the most important for our attendees to pay attention to?" A bit confused by the question, John said, "All of them are important. That's why they are on the list." By the end of John's presentation, more than 90 percent of the online attendees had left the meeting. It was after this embarrassing experience that John reached out for help. After watching the recording of his presentation, it was evident where he went astray. Not one slide contained an image, and all were simply paragraphs or bulleted lists of text typed into 10 PowerPoint slides.

THREE VISUAL MISTAKES TO AVOID IN PRESENTATIONS

Imagery plays a vital role in conveying a presentation's message. Images transform ideas into something meaningful. They evoke emotions, causing your listeners to see themselves on a journey. And they provide the structure for the audience's imagination to flow in concert with the message you are sharing. The overwhelming majority of presentations will include slides, and the most popular presentation software is Microsoft PowerPoint. In our experience working with business professionals, there are three slide design mistakes that lead to presentation disaster. Avoid making these at all costs.

Mistake 1: Too Much Text on a Slide

No matter how often we advise clients to limit the text on a slide, they don't do it. The temptation to keep adding information to a slide is astonishing, but it's a habit you must break because text-filled slides render your presentation useless. The effectiveness of your presentation is not determined by what's on a slide, it's determined by what is *not* on the slide. Your slides don't carry your presentation, you do.

Brevity is key. Limit the content on a slide to one point. Avoid using more than three bullets on a slide. And where possible, replace text with an image.

Mistake 2: Ineffective Use of Color

We've all seen slides filled with colors that make the text unreadable. This happens for many reasons, including the presenter likes certain colors, the design must use the organization's brand colors, and the list goes on. There's a simple technique to avoid using bad color combinations: use contrast. The colors used in your slide background should always contrast with the font colors. This ensures your slides are legible.

Never use light-colored fonts on a light-colored background. As simple as that sounds, we see this mistake constantly. If you're not sure if the color combination you want to use is a good one, ask a friend or colleague. You can also use a color wheel to test color combinations. Our favorite online tool for testing color combinations is Canva's Color Wheel.[1]

Mistake 3: Font Size Is Too Small

When presenters try to add as much information to a slide as possible (remember mistake 1?), they keep reducing the font size to achieve that goal. In fact, when we've asked presenters what the smallest font size is they should use on a slide, more than 90 percent either did not know or answered incorrectly. The rule of thumb is a 24-point font or higher to ensure readability. The larger the room you are presenting in, the bigger the font should be to ensure people at the back can read your slides. Bigger is always better.

Top 3 Slide Design Mistakes

Too Much Text on a Slide

Limit the content on a slide to a single main point or concept.

Ineffective Use of Color

Use contrast to ensure fonts are legible on a slide.

Font Size Is Too Small

Use at least 24-point font to ensure slides can be read from any location in the room.

BASICS OF CREATING GREAT VISUALS

Finding the right visuals can be one of the most time-consuming tasks when constructing a presentation. There's a lot to consider. Will the image play a primary or supporting role in the presentation? What mood will the visual convey or evoke? How many images will be used on a slide? Will slides include animations and transitions?

The good news is you don't have to be a graphic designer to make a visually appealing slide deck. By following a few basic design tenets, you can create stunning visuals with ease. Let's see how this works.

Spacing and Alignment

When adding elements such as text and images to a slide, be mindful of how the reader's eyes will absorb the information. People typically read slides by starting in the top left corner and follow a Z pattern (from the top left to the bottom right). This offers presenters a wide array of spacing and alignment options to guide the reader's eyes. Making items of importance larger than other elements creates a natural hierarchy your readers unconsciously understand.

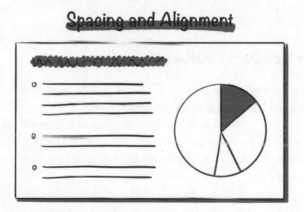

Contrast

As mentioned, contrast is an effective technique for creating visually appealing slides. Contrast can be accomplished by using different colors, using different images that contrast with one another, using larger and smaller elements on a slide, and so on. The options are limited only by your creativity and imagination. But remember, brevity is king. So, limit the number of elements on a slide because *less is always more*.

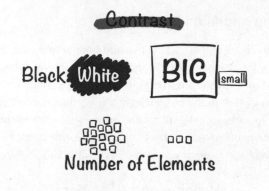

Typeface Classifications

It's quite common for presenters to use default fonts. This leads to readability challenges for your audience, and in many instances, you are completely unaware the problem exists simply based on your choice of font. Fonts are grouped together in a set known as a typeface. Generally, you'll use two different typefaces in a presentation: serif and sans serif.

Serif fonts are fonts with a small line or "tail" on the end of a letter. They have a sophisticated look. San serif fonts do not have that "tail." They look plain. So, which should you choose when selecting a font? In general, serif fonts (the fancy looking ones) have high readability for text applications. They are traditionally used in academic, editorial, and formal documents. San serif fonts generally have medium to high readability and are typically used for a more modern look and feel. They make great headings or headlines. Where presenters get into trouble is using script fonts. Despite being high impact, script fonts are exceedingly difficult to read in a presentation and should be avoided.

Following these basic tenets will help you create slides that look great and reinforce your message. But there's an easier way to create stunning visuals than having to remember the tenets.

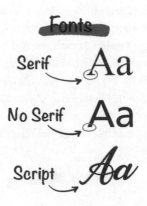

Templates Make You Look Great

Why try to design eye-popping slides when they've been designed for you? We're not talking about the templates native to PowerPoint or other presentation design software. We're talking about templates that are absolutely stunning. The graphic design industry has evolved from a high-cost, high-effort adventure into an industry focused on creating do-it-yourself designs for the everyday person. No longer do you have to outsource to an expert. They've made templates you can change in minutes using plug-and-play technology on an internet-connected device, including your smartphone.

At the time of writing this book, our favorite online graphic design tool is Canva. With millions—yes you read that right, *millions*—of images that can be dragged and dropped into hundreds of thousands of templates, this tool is the presenter's dream. Canva's library of assets is not limited to images either. It also contains ready-made video, audio, and other resources. It's at the top of our recommended tools list.

Other providers of high-impact, low-cost templates are widely available. HubSpot is another excellent source of digital assets. Their blog article, "The Free Design Templates You Need to Create Stunning Visual Marketing Content,"[2] contains a shocking array of free resources. There are nearly 400 templates available including templates for social media content, PowerPoint presentations, infographics, Canva, and more. HubSpot even includes more than 550 royalty-free stock photos. Conduct a simple Google search or contact your internal

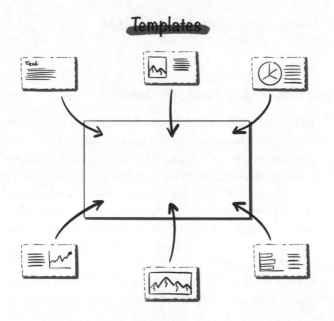

marketing department and they should be able to recommend some great options.

A final note. Always reach out to your local colleges and universities for assistance via interns. Don't feel like you have to do this alone. Great graphic design is easy and widely available at very affordable prices. You are just a click away from creating stunning visuals for your presentation.

A POORLY DESIGNED SLIDE DECK WILL DERAIL THE BEST OF PRESENTERS

Amy was a contract trainer who worked for several high-profile clients. Her favorite customer contacted her to work on a custom project for one of their clients, and she was thrilled. She had worked with her customer's client many years ago, which meant she was somewhat familiar with the organization. Her customer had an instructional designer who was creating a customized case study to use during the training. Amy was a well-respected facilitator, so her customer did not involve Amy in the actual design process. She was brought into the project meetings just a few days before the training was to begin. This was not unusual because Amy had taught the core course; all she needed to review was the details of the customized case study.

In the first project meeting Amy attended, she instantly noticed the slides for the customized case study were overflowing with text. She expressed concern that the amount of time allotted for the trainees to read the mountain of information was unrealistic. The instructional designer said she raised the same concern with the client, but the client provided the slides and did not want them changed. To Amy's dismay, the senior manager did not want to push back on the client at this stage of the process. After all, they had been working on the project for the past four weeks, and the class was scheduled to start next week. Amy reluctantly agreed to proceed as planned.

During the first training session, participants openly complained they were not given sufficient time to interpret the information. With their managers observing the class, Amy tried to manage the situation, but it was nosediving toward failure. Following the first session, the client's senior manager emailed Amy's customer expressing severe displeasure with the course. The senior manager wrote: "The instructor struggled with giving instructions and our people were confused throughout the entire session. We expect this to not be an issue in the next session." Amy didn't sleep after reading that email.

After the third of six scheduled virtual training sessions, the client decided to end the training. Amy was exhausted, distraught, and completely disappointed because she warned her customer this would happen. Her customer ultimately had to refund the fees for the customized course, and it left Amy with a loss of trust in her customer's willingness to listen to her feedback. Situations like Amy's are far too common, and it all boils down to an unwillingness to invest the time and effort to ensure your slide designs are not going to lead to presentation disaster. Using the techniques and strategies in this chapter and throughout this book, you'll avoid falling into the same traps.

• • •

Avoiding the most common mistakes as well as understanding and following the basics of creating good visuals will equip you to succinctly deliver your message in a memorable way. Use these tips to craft visually stunning images to capture your audience's attention like a pro.

ESSENTIAL TAKEAWAYS

- Strategically designing your visual aids will help communicate your Big Idea.

- Don't make these common mistakes when creating your visual aids: too much text, too many or ineffective color schemes, or too small text.

- Use good spacing and alignment, appropriate contrasting colors, and correct fonts and sizes.

- Use templates to easily create slides.

Making Your Presentations Unforgettable

Dear Presenter:

I'll get right to the point. I have only a few minutes to listen to your babble. The truth is, I live in the status quo for as long as I can, even if I'm unhappy with it, because to change requires a lot of me. And I hate that. Life is tough and I have a lot of distractions going on and limited bandwidth right now. I'm pretty busy with my priorities. Unless you surprise me, chances are ridiculously high that I'm going to find myself wishing I were doing something else. If you want me to listen to you, you've got to grab my attention. Make me feel what you're saying. Excite me to see what you're wanting me to see. Help me believe in a better future when we're done with this song-and-dance ritual called a presentation. If you do that, I promise I'll look up from my phone. I'll minimize the other windows on my computer. And if you do it enough, I'll pay attention to your entire presentation.

So, before you show your first slide. Before you say your first word. Think about me—your audience. I want you to make this time we have together memorable.

Sincerely,
Your Audience

THE CANDID TRUTH

As brutally honest as this letter might seem, it highlights an unfortunate reality every presenter must confront. Those in your audience are overworked, time-constrained, and suffering from attention overload. As hard as you might try, they will remember almost none of your entire presentation. So, if you want them to remember anything, you must say and do it in a way that causes their brains to pay attention. And you have one heck of a secret weapon for doing that: a memorable catchphrase.

A memorable catchphrase is an idea summarized in a sentence or two. And, while that may seem simple, actually executing a memorable catchphrase can be quite difficult. In fact, if you're not a student of writing, or copywriting in particular, memorable writing may not be a skill you've developed. Fortunately, much of what professional copywriters, marketers, and scriptwriters do to create those memorable catchphrases and one-liners is formulaic. In fact, almost all of the most famous lines from blockbuster movies are simply statements created using formulas. "My name is Bond. James Bond." "Yeah baby, yeah." "To be, or not to be." "Burn baby burn." "Home sweet home."

Do you see a pattern? These are figures of rhetoric that use the formula A-B-A. You say something (A), say something else (B), and repeat the first thing you said (A). Figures of rhetoric are statements used to convince an audience to agree with you, and they are what make messages sticky.

To Be Sticky Is to Be Simple

There are many different formulas for writing memorable phrases. Mark Forsyth's book *The Elements of Eloquence*[1] contains 39 formulas for crafting statements that could make you a legend. But we're going to show you a simple way for creating sticky statements. And the first rule of thumb is to keep it simple. If you can't make it simple, no one cares.

Remember the famous line, "Frankly, my dear, I don't give a damn," from the 1939 film *Gone with the Wind*? Keeping it simple shows your listener you care. Clarity is caring. Complexity is agonizing. Did you notice we dropped two potentially sticky catchphrases in the last five sentences? The first potentially sticky catchphrase is "If you don't make it simple, no one cares." The second potentially sticky catchphrase is "Clarity is caring. Complexity is agonizing." To be sticky, say it in as few words as possible.

CREATING MEMORABLE PHRASES WITH EASE

Very little in the world is new. Most is an improved version of the known. The same holds true for being memorable. The easiest path to creating sticky phrases is to use existing phrases as a form of inspiration. You can create unique catchphrases using well-known sayings or proverbs that express a perceived truth based on common sense or experience. Here are several examples of proverbs you already know:

A dog is a man's best friend.

Haste makes waste.

Garbage in, garbage out.

You can't have your cake and eat it, too.

With great power comes great responsibility.

If the shoe fits, wear it.

Don't count your chickens before they hatch.

Don't put all your eggs in one basket.

We'll cross that bridge when we come to it.

Ignorance is bliss.

With a little tweaking, you can create a new and potentially memorable phrase from these well-known proverbs:

Original: We'll cross that bridge when we come to it.

New phrase: Build the bridge that others want to cross.

Original: If the shoe fits, wear it.

New phrase: If the shoe doesn't fit, make a better shoe.

Original: Don't put all your eggs in one basket.

New phrase: Don't put all your eggs in one basket unless you only have one egg and one basket.

Original: Ignorance is bliss.

New phrase: Ignorance is not only bliss, it's contagious.

Seeing examples helps those creative juices flow. In fact, as we wrote this chapter, we created the following new sticky phrases:

- The greatest threat to humankind is the unkind human.

- To live is to love. To love is to live . . . poorly.

- On the internet, nobody knows you're stupid until you show them.

- Slow and steady wins last place at NASCAR.

Use as few words in a sentence as possible. That's the secret to writing a memorable catchphrase or one-liner.

MORE EXAMPLES OF GREAT CATCHPHRASES

There are many authors and speakers who are legendary for their pithy statements. Here are three of our favorites and just a few of their sticky phrases:

- John C. Maxwell, leadership expert and bestselling author

  o A crisis doesn't make your character, it reveals your character.[2]

  o Great leaders see more and see before.[3]

  o A lack of realism today costs credibility tomorrow.[4]

- I want to make a difference with people who want to make a difference doing something that makes a difference.[5]

- Add value to others so that they may multiply the value of others.[6]

• Craig Groeschel, pastor and host of the Craig Groeschel Leadership Podcast

- Imitation is born out of limitation.[7]

- It's the things no one sees that bring the results everyone wants.[8]

- Identity shapes actions.[9]

- Successful people do consistently what other people do occasionally.[10]

• James Clear, author of *Atomic Habits* (Avery)

- When making plans, think big. When making progress, think small.

- Try things until things come easily.

- Most people live in a world others have created for them.

- Make good habits inevitable and bad habits impossible.

- Most days, people would rather be wrong with the crowd than be right by themselves.

Here's a secret to creating your own catchphrase with ease. When reading books and works from others, document quotes that move and inspire you. Build a searchable database of quotes to find one that perfectly fits with your list. This tiny bit of extra effort is one of the habits of very charismatic presenters and speakers because it exponentially expands their word choices. You become charismatic simply by intentionally becoming more versed in word choice.

FIVE PLACES TO PLANT A CATCHPHRASE OR ONE-LINER IN PRESENTATIONS

Now that you know how to create catchphrases, it is time to figure out where to put them in your presentation. This is where the real fun begins in speech preparation because a memorable one-liner that convinces people to agree with you can be placed anywhere in your speech. This provides several opportunities to say something people will remember and repeat. Here are five excellent locations in your speech to plant a convincing, memorable one-liner.

1. After Telling a Story

Diana Damron, an author and expert in civility, offers keynotes, training programs, and executive coaching to organizations and leaders who wish to create a more civil workplace. We've had the pleasure of coaching Diana as a member of our online "Speak for a Living Success Academy" speaker coaching program, and one day during a session together the roles were reversed. Sardék sought Diana's expertise after a challenging situation he had experienced with a participant in one of his virtual training sessions. The participant verbally attacked Sardék on an open mic, using profane language and degrading comments that all participants could hear. The participant was upset because, as she put it, she was "not getting anything out of the course or from the facilitator [Sardék]." After hearing the situation, Diana provided excellent techniques for managing uncivil behavior like this. But what made her feedback so memorable was the single sentence she shared after Sardék told the story of his difficult participant experience. Diana said, "Incivility is the dark side of bad behavior." That was pure gold! Sardék not only had a story of intense incivility he could share in his future train-the-trainer and speaker-coaching sessions, he now also had a powerfully memorable one-liner to use (with author attribution) at the end of that story.

Here's the key to using one-liners at the end of a story. When telling a story with a great deal of significance to the overall message of your presentation, be sure the point for telling it is extremely clear. Then create or find a one-liner that convinces the audience to agree with you and the point you made by telling the story. That's all you need to do. Remember, too, you don't need a memorable one-liner for every story you tell. You only need a memorable one-liner for *the most important* stories you tell.

2. As a Title or Section Header

Open any book and you'll see chapter after chapter contains a memorable one-line chapter title. "Walk Slowly, but Never Backward" is the title of Chapter 11 in James Clear's bestseller *Atomic Habits*.[11] "Start with Why, But Know How" is Chapter 8's title in Simon Sinek's *Start with Why*.[12] And our personal favorite chapter title comes from the authors of *Influencer*,[13] in which Chapter 4 is titled "Help Them Love What They Hate."

Just as one-liners set the tone in a book, they can also set the tone for your presentation. As you transition from one main point to the next, use a catchphrase to open or close a section. Place it on a slide.

Reference it in the handout you provide. And if the quote is in the form of a question, you'll grab the audience's attention for both the novelty and intrigue posed by the quote.

3. After a List

Lists are a presenter's best friend, allowing you to communicate information in a very succinct manner. Whenever you have a particularly important list, deploy a catchphrase to make it worth remembering. In presentations based on her book *True North: A Four-Week Approach to Ignite Your Passion and Activate Your Potential*, Anne shares a list of four steps for completing week one activities. She then shares this great one-liner to inspire her audience to act: "You can't be anything you want, but you can be anything you're capable of becoming." Invest a little time and research in crafting or finding a quote that reinforces the message of the list, and you raise the potential for your audience to repeat it to others after your presentation.

4. As a Tagline

"We're not retailers with a mission, we're missionaries who retail" is an awesome one-liner said by CEO John Mackey when he described what makes Whole Foods different from other retailers. If you've ever stayed at a Ritz-Carlton hotel, you may have heard, "We are ladies and gentlemen serving ladies and gentlemen." These are examples of taglines—catchphrases or slogans used in marketing. Typically three to six words in length, taglines are extremely popular for their stickiness. Due to their brevity, they are moderately difficult to create. While you can and should try creating your own, there are online tools that

can help, such as Shopify's free slogan maker (https://www.shopify
.com/tools/slogan-maker).

You can also ask someone in your marketing or communications
department to help craft a tagline or provide authorization to use an
existing tagline in your presentation.

5. At the Close to Your Presentation

A memorable quote is a fantastic way to end a presentation. It can be
used in conjunction with a call to action to form an intensely provocative moment.

During the close to his keynote speech to the US Department of
Housing and Urban Development (HUD), Sardék shared a story about
Elsa Garcia Russo. The story began with the first time he met Elsa. He
met Elsa when he arrived at the Mexico City airport, where he had trav-
eled to deliver a keynote speech for the Association for Talent Development Mexico Summit. She was the greeter, and in a very short period
of time, they formed a connection. Sardék and his wife took an extra
couple of days to tour Mexico City, and Elsa accompanied them because she wanted to ensure they got a proper taste of Mexican culture.
A true friendship was born between Elsa and the Loves. She would
soon be moving to the United States to marry the love of her life, and
Sardék and his wife visited Elsa and her fiancé multiple times. Heart-
breakingly, just six months after meeting Elsa, she was diagnosed with
terminal cancer and died. Sardék and his wife were absolutely devas-
tated by the loss of this beautiful angel who had so much energy and
so much life to live.

Pausing as he struggled to hold back tears at that point in the
story during his HUD keynote speech, Sardék said, "There are times in
your life when you meet someone who completely changes your life.

Someone who inspires you to live a better life. I hope by telling you Elsa Garcia Russo's story that you are inspired just as I was. Because you, HUD, you make a difference in the lives of so many. So, I ask you, What are you going to do to make a difference in the lives of the people you will never meet and the children who have not been born yet?"

That closing line—"What are you going to do to make a difference in the lives of the people you will never meet and the children who have not been born yet?"—was moving. It was the perfect call to action to all of the HUD leaders and staff who were responsible for making decisions that affect millions of Americans after a story that showed just how impactful their roles could really be.

When closing your presentation, say something memorable. Say something inspiring. Say something worth repeating. Say something that ignites the spark of action. If you do that—and we assure you that you can—you will live on in the minds and hearts of all who were fortunate to hear you.

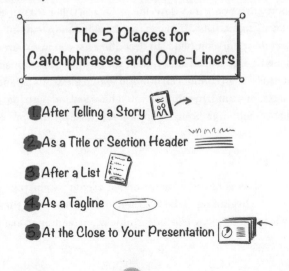

The 5 Places for Catchphrases and One-Liners

1. After Telling a Story
2. As a Title or Section Header
3. After a List
4. As a Tagline
5. At the Close to Your Presentation

OTHER LANGUAGE TOOLS TO CREATE MEMORABLE CATCHPHRASES AND ONE-LINERS

It can be daunting to try to figure out how to use the many different language tools to create memorable statements. Realistically, you just need to use a few time-tested tools to be perceived as a charismatic, persuasive presenter. Here are three of our favorites; refer to this list whenever you want to create a sticky statement for your presentation.

Alliteration

Alliteration is the repetition of a letter or sound at the beginning of words. You've been overexposed to alliterations in marketing and advertising campaigns. It's not hard to envision you seeing a coffee shop describe its brand of specialty coffee as "sweet, smooth, and satisfying." An amusement park may describe its biggest roller coaster as "totally and terrifyingly terrific." You can use the alliteration "carefully curated to be concise and complete" to describe a list you just shared in your presentation. To use an alliteration, start with the letter or sound you want to use. Then conduct an internet search for words that begin with that letter or sound. In minutes you'll have several potential words to craft an attention-grabbing, memorable phrase for your presentation.

Anadiplosis

Anadiplosis is using a word at the end of a sentence and repeating that word at the beginning of the next sentence. You've seen these before and will instantly recognize the formula when reading an example. For example, Sardék used anadiplosis to create what he calls the Priority Principle. The Priority Principle states: Questions create priorities. Priorities create action. Action creates results. As soon as people hear it, they immediately start writing it down, so when he says it, he repeats it to give audiences time to capture it in their notes. Here are two examples we made up:

- Joy leads to happiness. Happiness leads to success. Success leads to freedom.

- Repetition is a requirement for overcoming failure. Failure is a requirement for achieving success.

Anadiplosis is incredibly easy to create. With a little practice, you can craft really interesting quotes by simply repeating a word from the end of one sentence at the beginning of the next.

Chiasmus

Chiasmus is the repeating of a phrase, with the order of the words reversed. John F. Kennedy said one of the most famous chiasmus during his 1961 inaugural address. He said, "Ask not what your country can do for you. Ask what you can do for your country."[14] Maybe you've heard the three musketeers' famous line, "One for all and all for one."

A chiasmus is relatively easy to create. Simply write a phrase and then write it in reverse order. Put the two phrases together and refine the wording until it makes sense.

Here are a few examples:

- Just as the staff supported our leaders in difficult times, in difficult times our leaders must support our staff.

- Success requires growth just as growth requires change.

- We never compete on price, and we never let price prevent us from competing.

In each example, the result is a statement that the audience can agree with. Don't worry if the second phrase is not an exact mirror in reverse of your first phrase as is the case in our compete on price example. So, practice using the general formula for a chiasmus and you're likely to create a very intriguing, persuasive phrase.

PRACTICE DOESN'T MAKE PERFECT, PERFECT PRACTICE MAKES PROFICIENT

You never get good at anything without practicing your way there. This is true with writing memorable catchphrases, too. The technique requires practice, and the more you practice, the dramatically better you'll get at creating them.

One final tip (in a memorable place at the end of the chapter, we might add) when writing phrases, write as many versions as you can. This allows you to develop the habit of continuous refinement. That single habit will enable you to become very efficient at writing until you identify the version that naturally stands out. The only thing standing between your presentation being memorable and a standing ovation is you.

So, start writing. Enjoy the process. And, be memorable.

ESSENTIAL TAKEAWAYS

- Use pithy catchphrases and one-liners in your presentations to stay relevant and memorable.

- Audiences are time-strapped and short on attention; make your messages stick.

- Follow the A-B-A formula to create a catchphrase and keep it simple.

- Put a new spin on an old proverb to update it for today's audiences.

- You don't need a memorable one-liner for every story you tell, just for the *most important* stories you tell.

- Plant a catchy phrase in any of the five recommended places during your presentation: after telling a story, as a title or header, after a list, as a tagline, and as the close to your presentation.

Climactic
Closers

You've reached the end of the presentation. All of your hard work
and preparation has brought you to this point. Perhaps you've poured
your soul into sharing your message. Maybe you're just thankful for
surviving this speaking or corporate presentation experience. Or perhaps you're somewhere in between.

What matters most now is to bring the session to a close. Not just
any close. Not just with a wave, a nod, and an audible "Thank you." This
is your last opportunity to make a difference—to make your message
worthy of being remembered and inspiring enough to be acted upon.
Thankfully, closing a presentation in a climactic way is easy when you
follow our proven four-step process.

We coach presenters to work through this process, and like them,
your presentation will end with the audience standing in line waiting
to thank you for investing in them and adding value.

POWERFUL CONCLUSIONS MADE EASY FORMULA

If you've done the work to prepare a presentation and are ready to con-struct a climactic close, here's how to do it.

Step 1: Tell a Short Story to Begin Your Close

Brené Brown began the close of her TEDx KC talk, "The Price of Invul-nerability," with a final story: "Here's what I learned from the research. We practice gratitude. We stop and be thankful for what we have. I've interviewed a lot of people who have been through many horrific things, from genocide to trauma. And when you ask them what they need, they will tell you—I don't need your pity, I don't need your sym-pathy. I need to know when you look at your children, I need to know you are grateful. I need to know you know what you have. So, to prac-tice gratitude. To honor what's ordinary about our lives because that is what's truly extraordinary."[1] Brené's final words show why it's impor-tant to tell a short, final story. It allows you to evoke the emotions that drive your audience to act. It reminds them why they listened and why they should act. It's also a lead-in for your call to action.

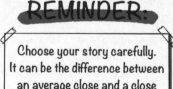

REMINDER:

Choose your story carefully. It can be the difference between an average close and a close your audience never forgets.

Step 2: Summarize Your Key Points

You've just told a final story. In fact, you've told stories and shared examples throughout your presentation to build the case for your audience to take action. By following that presentation structure, you've been selling your idea all along. Before you ask the audience to do something (known as your call to action), you need to remind them of what you've told them by summarizing your key points. In a minute or less, restate each of your key points followed by a transition question to connect your key points to your call to action. Here's an example.

In his keynote "Leading with Impact," Sardék takes the audience on a highly engaging journey using a variety of activities as he teaches the five components of his leadership model. After telling his final story, he simply recaps the journey by summarizing the model's five components. Nothing special, unique, or complicated. Then he uses a transition question to move to the call to action. "Can you see how easy it is to engage and effectively lead your teams using these simple, commonsense tactics?" The transition question is designed to elicit a yes response from the audience. Asking such a question increases audience buy-in and reduces any resistance to your ideas. Asking a transition question may be new to you, so here are several examples to use in your presentations:

- Isn't it exciting when you finally see how this all comes together?

- Can you imagine how great it's going to feel when you . . . ?

- Aren't you ready to put this into action right now?

- Are you feeling a sense of relief now that you know you don't have to [add the pain point you helped them overcome]?

- See how easy it was to . . . ?

- How far can we go and how fast can we grow knowing what we know now?

For more examples, pay attention at the end of promotional webinars, and you'll be able to easily identify the transition question.

Remember, you're using the transition question to set the audience up for the call to action, so use a bit of trial and error to find the right wording that feels comfortable to you and your style. Do that, and you're ready to move to the most important step in a climactic close—the call to action.

Step 3: State Your Call to Action

Alan Stein Jr. is world-renowned for helping elite athletes like professional basketball players Steph Curry, Kevin Durant, and late great Kobe Bryant achieve peak performance. While being interviewed on the *Ed Mylett Show*,[3] he recounted when in 2007 he watched Kobe's famous 4 a.m. off-season workouts. Alan remembers being shocked at the simplicity of what Kobe was doing—things like basic pivoting and footwork skills—not exactly what you would expect from one of the best NBA players ever. At the end of the workout, Alan said to Kobe, "I don't get it. You are the best player in the world. Why are you doing such basic drills?" Kobe gave him a friendly smile and a wink and responded, "Why do you think I am the best player in the world? Because I never get bored with the basics."

That remarkable story left the listeners wanting to hear more. By doing that, Alan flawlessly had hooked the podcast audience and spent the rest of the interview building the case for reading Alan's book to learn the techniques for achieving peak performance. When they came to the close of the interview, the call to action was insanely clear. Ed Mylett said, "I want everybody to go get *Sustain Your Game*." That's it. There was no guesswork involved. Ed told the audience exactly what he wanted them to do. That's what you need to do, too. Tell the audience exactly what you want them to do. Be very clear, and don't leave it to their imagination. If you want them to sign up for an offer, tell them to sign up. If you want them to show a coworker some form of gratitude each day, tell them to do it.

This is the climax of your presentation. If you've done your job, your audience is ready to take action. All that is left is to inspire them to take action by using the fourth and final step of the climactic close process.

Step 4: End with an Inspirational Quote or Catchphrase

Whether you use a quote written by someone else or craft your own inspirational quote using the tips and techniques in Chapter 8, closing with a quote shows your audience you cared enough to find words meant just for them. And when done extremely well, the audience will display the ultimate show of appreciation—sometimes a standing ovation.

ESSENTIAL TAKEAWAYS

- Your closing phrase is your final opportunity to make a difference.

- Use your closer to drive home your Big Idea.

- Follow the four-step proven process to craft your closer: tell a short story to begin your close, summarize your key points, state your call to action, and end with an inspirational quote or catchphrase.

Delivering Online Content

Beginning in 2020, our global society quickly shifted to conducting business online—and presenting virtually became a monumental part of that change. In fact, nothing puts this earth-shattering transformation into perspective better than these Zoom statistics before and after April 2020.

Daily Meeting Participants		Annual Revenue	
December 2019	10 million	2019	$623 million
April 2020	300 million	2020	$2.6 billion

Source: The Business of Apps, https://www.businessofapps.com/data/zoom-statistics/.

Organizations and their leaders struggled to manage in this unprecedented crisis, and thanks to high-speed connections and specialty software programs like Zoom, Microsoft Teams, and others, delivering content online quickly became a new business model for many organizations, educators, and individuals.

In this chapter, we'll review the best practices regarding the equipment and resources required to effectively deliver an engaging presentation online. Let's begin by reviewing the hardware you'll need.

LIGHTS, MICS, CAMERAS, SCREENS, ACTION!

When delivering a presentation online or in a hybrid format, many presenters assume standard-issued equipment is sufficient. But this assumption ignores the significant variations in the quality of delivery that inevitably happen when working from the office versus from home. Use the following recommendations as a checklist to assess your current level of readiness.

Lights

Lighting is easy to overlook, especially when working remotely. Using natural light from windows or using lights from lamps is rarely going to produce a quality on-screen experience for your audience. It's important to set up external lights to eliminate shadows and illuminate your face properly. There are many options available that include a wide variety of ring lights, desk-attached lights, and stand-alone studio-type lighting kits. They are inexpensive, easy to set up, and necessary for reinforcing presenter credibility.

Mics

A mic is the one piece of equipment most presenters don't have because they don't realize how much of a difference an external mic has on audio quality. This is so significant that after Sardék demonstrates the difference in audio quality to program attendees in his "Master Virtual Presenter" program, every member who has watched the video purchases an external mics. Like external cameras, external mics come in many varieties and are universally available, so conduct some research to determine the best fit based on your price point and individual needs.

Cameras

Modern laptops and Apple products include cameras as a standard feature. However, the quality of the camera can vary widely, and it's very common to see pixelated or grainy video from internal cameras. We recommend presenters use an external high-definition camera that is readily available from local and online retailers. The technology is changing rapidly, so do some research before making a purchase. A Google search for the best external cameras or a visit to a local retailer who specializes in external camera products will help you make the right choice.

Screens

One major lesson learned from transitioning to virtual and hybrid presentations is the need for multiple computer screens. You will be frustrated if you only have one screen because it is nearly impossible to properly manage and deliver a virtual presentation from a single screen. We recommend having at least one external monitor that can serve as a second screen to extend application windows from your computer. For those who present frequently online, two external monitors are recommended. Three total screens provides the greatest flexibility and ease of managing a virtual presentation.

• • •

Delivering virtual presentations requires a great deal of planning simply because you are expected to deliver the same audience experience . . . without an audience in front of you. But, with the right equipment and resources, a memorable virtual presentation is absolutely possible. We realize some organizations don't provide the external equipment we recommend and that's incredibly unfortunate. But, think of it this way: your employer owns your job title; you own your career. Investing in resources that further your career will pay off—so go ahead and invest in yourself by purchasing the equipment you need.

ADDITIONAL VIRTUAL PRESENTATION REQUIREMENTS

While your equipment is the entry price into the game of virtual presentations, there are other considerations that affect your level of success. Let's look at those.

Virtual Platforms

Zoom, Microsoft Teams, Webex, and Adobe Connect are just a few of the many platforms used to deliver online presentations. While all platforms offer standard features such as chat, session recording, and more, there are differences that affect the level of interactivity you can have with virtual participants. With the rapid pace of development of these tools, it is critical to become intimately familiar with the platforms used by your organization and your clients. For speakers, this is especially true because the platforms used for large-scale events can be significantly different from those more commonly used for smaller meetings.

It can be time consuming to stay on top of the latest tech enhancements for each platform. Ask your IT department for assistance or do an online search for the platform that best suits your requirements. Many of our clients' IT departments created quick reference charts their employees can use to compare platforms supported by the organization. You can also subscribe to the newsletter for the platforms you use, allowing you to stay up to date with any changes. Finally, use your professional network for guidance. Posting questions on LinkedIn is a very effective way to crowdsource answers to questions.

Working with Producers

Delivering a presentation online to a potentially global audience comes with some inherit challenges. Technology and infrastructure stability is a major barrier. It can be daunting to attempt to manage the tech and administration of the event while also delivering your presentation. This is the top reason why we suggest having a producer work alongside you during your presentation. Producers typically provide behind-the-scenes tech and customer service support, freeing you to focus solely on delivering a great presentation. Producers can also copresent or facilitate the content with you.

Be Prepared and Keep Backup Resources

It was 6 p.m. Sunday evening. Sardék was reviewing his slides because it was the night before he was scheduled to fly to Orlando to deliver his signature "Facilitating with Impact!" workshop at the 2022 *Training Magazine* annual conference. Suddenly, his laptop's screen turned blue. In a flash, his main hard drive crashed, rendering his laptop completely inoperable. In a panic, he pulled out an old laptop, connected to his cloud-based file backup system, and began downloading the backup files to his old laptop. To his astonishment, it was going to take 36 hours to complete the download. He didn't have 36 hours. He had less than 10. This exposed a significant vulnerability in his business continuity plan, and he immediately purchased a brand-new second laptop that is now continuously synchronized with his main one to ensure he always has a ready-to-go backup system. The message of this story is clear—back up everything, and always have a backup available of everything you need to deliver a presentation. This includes having a mobile Wi-Fi option if your main Wi-Fi goes down.

HOW TO ENGAGE A VIRTUAL AUDIENCE

Now that you understand the tools and other resources required to deliver an effective virtual presentation, let's examine what it takes to engage a virtual audience. The principles of audience engagement are the same for an in-person audience and a virtual audience. The difference lies in the tools used for engagement. As we'll discuss, there is a massive challenge when it comes to keeping virtual audiences engaged.

From March 2020 through April 2022, Sardék Love International consistently surveyed more than 1,600 global training professionals to identify the top challenge they experience when delivering live virtual instructor-led training. After every survey, a lack of participant engagement ranked as the number one challenge for trainers, consistently by a 2-to-1 margin over the second ranked challenge.

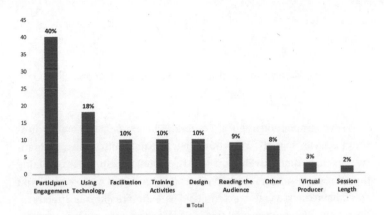

**Top Challenges Trainers Say They Are Facing
When Delivering Training Online**
Source: Sardék Love International Survey

This exposes a significant problem with live virtual presentations and training sessions. It is very common to attend an online presentation delivered with little-to-no participant interaction, and that leads to the presentation becoming nothing more than an information dumping session. When this happens, it creates what Sardék has coined as the "monologue with hostages" syndrome. This causes virtual audiences to turn their cameras off and begin multitasking, ignoring you and your content. So, what is the solution? How do you engage your participants during a live virtual presentation? The solution is to use the "law of engagement," which says engagement always begins with a question.

To keep people engaged, repeatedly pose questions to your participants and have them respond using any of the following standard virtual platform interaction tools:

- Chat

- Emoticon

- Text (such as annotating on the screen or whiteboard)

- Polls and surveys

For example, you might ask online participants: "How many countries have you visited?" You could then instruct them to post their answer in chat. Alternatively, you could ask them to respond by selecting their answer from a multiple-choice option in a poll or survey. Or you could have them use the text tool and type their responses directly on the screen. Engaging participants online follows this simple formula:

> Ask a question and have participants respond
> using an interaction tool.
>
> Do this repeatedly and you've established the
> basic foundation for creating an engaging
> online experience.

Becoming proficient at delivering highly engaging online presentations requires training in facilitation skills, so if you've never been trained in facilitation, we encourage you to attend a train-the-trainer course such as Sardék's "Master Virtual Presenter" program (www.mastervirtualpresenter.com) or a virtual facilitation course from the Association for Talent Development (www.td.org).

• • •

This chapter covered everything you need to successfully deliver content online, including the minimum tech tools you should have: external lights, mics, cameras, and screens. We reviewed the importance of developing proficiency using virtual platforms, working with a producer, and creating a backup system of your software and files. Finally, we provided a basic overview of facilitation skills by introducing the law of engagement.

ESSENTIAL TAKEAWAYS

- Virtual and hybrid presentations are becoming a new standard for effectively presenting inclusive content.

- Consider acquiring the following additional hardware for virtual presentations: good lighting, an external microphone, a high-definition camera, and multiple screens.

- Consider the platform format and interactivity levels for participants, working with a professional producer, and keeping backup resources.

- Invest in yourself to ensure you have the knowledge, skills, and resources required for delivering engaging virtual presentations.

CHAPTER

11

Developing a Signature Style

Often when we think of style, we think of what we wear and how we present our outer selves to the world. Developing your signature style for giving a presentation is similar because you're not only presenting your topic but also yourself and your unique way of communicating. Your signature style is an external expression of your character and personality and is reflected in how you present—whether you're an energetic extrovert who can bring down the house or a soft-spoken introvert with a calm demeanor and a knack for delivering just the facts. Tapping into your best attributes will power you through to presentation success.

Signature delivery styles generally fall into one of four categories: people-oriented, idea-oriented, process-oriented, or action-oriented. Some of these styles make emotional connections with an audience, whereas others persuade by using facts, analysis, and data to make the case. For example, if you're a *people-oriented* storyteller, you may excel at tugging at your audience's heartstrings. If your style leans toward the innovative *idea-oriented*, you may find success collaborating and brainstorming with others. Maybe you're great at distilling your message into easily digestible pieces; then your style is more *process-oriented*. An *action-oriented* style focuses on achieving objectives and results; it helps get the job done.

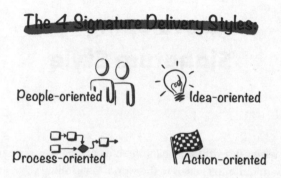

The 4 Signature Delivery Styles:

People-oriented

Idea-oriented

Process-oriented

Action-oriented

Whatever your style, make sure it's audience appropriate. You don't want to talk over your audience's level of understanding nor appear condescending. Always remember the end goal: you're presenting your message to solve a challenge, concern, or problem. Remain flexible with your style and adapt it as necessary. There are times when you may be required to adjust your delivery to fit the content of your presentation or your audience. If your signature style is casual, light-hearted, loud, and funny and the content of your presentation is more serious, tone down your delivery. For example, if you're giving a eulogy or your presentation is about the scourge of drunk driving, chances are you're not going to crack a joke. Knowing your presentation content as well as your audience are paramount considerations when it comes to your signature delivery.

This chapter looks at distinctly different examples of presenters, including Anne, with very different but equally effective signature styles. These examples show the full spectrum of signature styles from energetically extroverted to introspectively introverted to grace under pressure. The styles reflect the presenters' individual personalities, which they all use to their great advantage.

By developing a signature style, you'll be reinforcing connections with your audience. At the same time, you'll be improving your ability to read the room so you can deliver your message appropriately and meeting your goal of informing, instructing, entertaining, or persuading.

YOUR STYLE IS YOUR PERSONAL BRAND

Your style is largely based on your personality, relatability to the audience, and ability to engage an audience. It's your calling card and your reputation is based on it. Your signature style of presenting will grow from your personality and evolve from there, and, as already mentioned, you'll learn to adapt it depending on your content, situation, and audience. Presenting with a style all your own helps you convey your messages as well as make positive, memorable impressions on your audience. You can be one of the smartest people in the room, but without relating to your audience, you risk losing your credibility with them. Simply put, engage your audience with your style regardless of the content you're presenting or you'll lose their attention.

Think of the four styles mentioned: people-oriented, idea-oriented, process-oriented, and action-oriented. Which of these speaks to you the loudest or feels the most comfortable for you? It's got to feel good to look good. Knowing yourself well is important when developing your signature style. When thinking about the kind of style you have, it's also helpful to understand your ability to build relationships and be approachable. As the subject matter expert doing the presenting, you want your audience to come to you with questions, comments, and concerns. You don't want to appear intimidating or that you want to get off the stage as quickly as possible.

Not sure which of the styles you lean toward? Try videoing yourself or ask someone to video you as you present; then ask a trusted friend or colleague to gently critique your performance. Coaches are also available who specialize in helping presenters by giving constructive feedback to help you refine your style and method of presenting. It's a worthwhile investment if you plan to make a career in presentations.

An Example of Signature Style and Branding: Time Blocking with a Smile

One of the best, most fun signature styles we've seen was facilitated by life stylist Angie Quitasol when she created, wrote, and delivered her e-learning program "Time Blocking with a Smile." The program sold out almost immediately. Angie is the author of the book *Let's Do This: A Good Vibes Guide to Finding Your Inner Beat*. Her vibrant personality and energy sizzle right through the screen. It takes a special energy to present virtually to keep audiences engaged, and Angie is a master at virtual presentations.

Angie's "Time Blocking with a Smile" presentation is a great example of how to showcase your personal brand. She's been known to dance her way onto the stage to the sound of bass-thumping, energetic music. With her smiley-face brand front and center,

Angie—a former teacher, real estate agent, and lover of all things fun and funky—uses her teaching skills to share time management techniques with her lively and enthusiastic personal style and her skills from her real estate days to sell, sell, sell her programming. Angie teaches audiences the importance of setting goals and scheduling time to work toward them because out of sight is tantamount to not achieving what you want out of life. Says Angie, "If you schedule time to work on your goals, you're more likely to follow through." Check her out at StylebyAngieQ.com.

SIGNATURE STYLE PERSONIFIED

Dr. Sam Adeyemi, author of *Dear Leader: Your Flagship Guide to Successful Leadership*, never thought he would take the world stage with his presentations, but that's exactly what happened. In fact, he's a self-professed introvert who has been building an international movement since he was a young man in Africa.

With his warm smile and engaging welcome, his signature style presentation emits his approachability and relatability. Both are powerful presentation tools that have taken him to hundreds of countries, inspiring tens of thousands of people to build a better world by beginning with themselves, their values, and their own daily behaviors and treatment toward others. He not only asks this of his audiences; he requires it from himself and his teams. If you ask, he'll tell you this is all an organic and natural expression of his belief in a better planet and one humanity.

The point here is that his signature style drives his presentations, and to a large degree, his personal and professional success. His style is soft-spoken but powerful, and that's hugely impactful for his audiences. In online and in-person deliveries, his consistent and genuine approach displays his ability to gently but convincingly convey a message of values-based leadership. Throughout this chapter, we're using Dr. Sam, as he's called, as an example to demonstrate just what a signature style is and can look like.

YOUR SIGNATURE STYLE IN ACTION

Like Dr. Sam, you demonstrate your signature style with every presentation you deliver, through your tone, words, attitude, gestures, and even the content of your messages. For instance, in the "fireside chats" he posts on his social media, Dr. Sam leans slightly forward in his chair and speaks softly, projecting his warmth and authenticity as he shares his message of leading with positive values. His presentations instruct others to teach their followers' followers to become leaders as they move upward and onward in the spirit of "pay it forward." His presentation style exudes the same personal ideals he holds dear, and is an expression of his positive attitude, work ethic, character, and core values. The way he sees it—and we do, too—the job of a powerful presenter is to bring out the best in others so they can achieve success, in whatever form it takes.

CUSTOMIZE YOUR STYLE FOR EVERY PRESENTATION

As noted, you may encounter times where you need to adjust your style to be sensitive to the content, audience, or medium you are using to present. This customization requires a little flexibility, creativity, and even personal evolution on your part. As you develop your presentation skills, you'll grow your understanding of and experience in how to read your audience and customize your style with minor adjustments when appropriate.

Dr. Sam's style has developed over time and geography. Starting with humble beginnings in a small African village, Dr. Sam began his career as a presenter by serving as a minister to small groups near his home. He later established a school for leadership, and he now presents in more than 130 countries to more than 400,000 attendees at premiere events like the Global Leadership Summit. Over the years, he learned the value of customizing his delivery to his audience and adjusting his messaging—but not his energy—to fit the audience, venue, and medium in which he's presenting. You can visit him at GlobalLeadership.org or SamAdeyemi.com.

Keep Your Style (and Cool) Even in the Most Challenging Situations

Even the most easygoing presenters can get rattled when delivering a presentation. Early in Anne's speaking career, she was presenting for a small business group. Before she took the stage, attendees were treated to an open bar. By the time Anne took the stage and began her presentation, attendees were still enjoying dinner and drinks . . . many drinks.

Earlier that day, she had also participated in a controversial business interview on a popular radio talk show, and she knew that some people in the audience might have listened to the interview and had different opinions on the topic.

A man in the first row, who probably had been overserved, started heckling her just after she began her presentation. He loudly shouted a few insults at her, which Anne ignored. In the blink of an eye, she felt something hit the lapel of her white silk suit—it was a tomato from this man's entrée. The room went silent. Then, cool and collected, Anne looked down at the stain on her suit. She paused, swiped her index finger over where the tomato had hit her shoulder, scooped a morsel off her jacket, and dramatically tasted it.

"Hmmm. Needs more salt."

The silent crowd now roared with laughter, breaking the awkward tension. The chairman and cochair "escorted" the drunk man from the room.

By staying calm and using decorum, Anne turned the tables on the heckler and then took and kept control of the room. Although the situation was embarrassing, she let the audience take care of the situation and continued her presentation to a standing ovation.

OTHER SIGNATURE STYLE TIPS

There are several universal truths spanning all signature styles that point back to your main reason for presenting: inform, instruct, entertain, or persuade. Your style is how you deliver in a way that is uniquely you, and makes your message memorable. Use these tips for developing and demonstrating your style:

- **Know your audience.** Make sure your delivery is audience-appropriate. You're not going to tell an off-color joke to a church group, and you probably wouldn't explain the necessity of filing your income taxes to a preschool class. You want your presentation to be remembered for the right reasons. Take into consideration your audience's age, education, culture, comfort level with the subject matter, and what need of theirs you are filling with your message. Tell an appropriate story that allows your message to be heard. Facts tell, stories sell.

- **Connect with your audience.** Forging a connection is key to your believability and to how well your message is received. You may be speaking to a room of 5 or 5,000 people, but you're really just having a conversation. Approach your task as if you were speaking to one person. Focus on conversing with one person and then move to the next person; do so across the room. Read the room, and if your audience isn't connecting with your message or is missing your point, you can momentarily pause and reconnect by reiterating your point. Approach your communication with a heart of service. Remember that you want to get it right, and not necessarily be right. There's a big difference.

- **Get to know your audience.** Aside from connecting with your audience while you are on the stage, it's also important to get to know your audience *off* the stage, too. One way to do this is with meet and greets, which are also great for audience connectivity. This can work in a variety of ways. Typically the evening before the presentation, there is a mixer or group gathering. As the presenter, it's nice to attend these and meet your audience in person before the actual event takes place. You can also meet informally at a breakfast or by shaking hands with people at the door as they arrive or by releasing a brief looking-forward-to-meeting-you video a few days before your presentation. Any of these efforts will help cement your relationships as a friendly and approachable presenter.

- **Keep it simple and sincere.** Remember to *keep it simple and sincere*—our version of KISS. Authenticity and sincerity are key to audience connection. If your audience doubts your legitimacy, they'll stop listening and you'll lose all credibility. You don't want to be perceived as insincere or, worst of all, fake, because perception is reality when the spotlight is on you. Communicate from both your head and heart by knowing your subject matter and by delivering your message with positivity and energy. Let go of perfection and aim for proficiency. You can only control what you say, act, or feel. Then practice, practice, practice.

- **Emulate positive attributes of others.** Think about memorable speeches you've heard. How did those speakers capture your attention? Would that same practice work for you? Emulate the spirit of someone you admire to help you get your message across—as long as it's something you believe in and is authentically you, it will help you lock in your message. Practice storytelling in front of a mirror, your family, even your pet.

- **Have your end goal in mind.** Are you informing, instructing, entertaining, or persuading? What's the emotion you want your audience to feel or the action you want them to take? Have a beginning, middle, and end to your story. Know your call to action and reverse-engineer your story with this in mind.

• • •

Just as the style of your clothes reflects your culture, personality, or mood, how you create and develop your signature style for your presentations is what will set you apart from others—and what will potentially help get you invited back to present again and again. Your style is your brand. How you adapt your delivery to fit the event influences how the audience receives and processes your information. But it doesn't stop there. Ask yourself, "How will my audience respond to what I have to say and how I say it?" Their response becomes the real measure of your presentation's success.

ESSENTIAL TAKEAWAYS

- Your signature style is your personal brand.
- Signature styles vary and include people-oriented, idea-oriented, process-oriented, or action-oriented. They are as unique as the presenters themselves.
- Keep your signature style adaptable and flexible so you can customize your delivery to accommodate different content and presentation types.

CHAPTER

12

Delivering a Speech

Being invited to give a speech is exciting. It's a recognition that you possess a level of experience and expertise others feel is worth sharing. By its very nature, a speech is a high-stakes entry into the spotlight where all eyes are on you. That can be super exhilarating or ridiculously terrifying.

When coaching presenters on the process of preparing a speech, we typically uncover two obstacles we have to help them overcome. The first obstacle is helping them understand the difference between a speech and a presentation. The second is not having a process to manage preparing the speech. This chapter explores both obstacles.

THE DIFFERENCES BETWEEN SPEECHES AND PRESENTATIONS

This common confusion is likely because the terms "speech" and "presentation" are used interchangeably. There are some key differences, though, and the following table identifies 10 of these differences.

Differences Between a Speech and a Presentation

Speech	Presentation
Little emphasis on using visual aids to convey the message	Emphasis on using visual aids to convey the message
Focus on precise timing when conveying each key point	Focus on completing the presentation in the allotted time
Heavy emphasis on the spoken word, including the extensive use of metaphors, analogies, and storytelling	Low to moderate emphasis on the spoken word and use of analogies, metaphors, and storytelling
Typically scripted	Typically outlined but not scripted
Extensive rehearsal required	Moderate level of rehearsal required
Goal: shape how people think or feel about a topic	Goal: inform, educate, entertain, or persuade the audience
Heavy use of vocal variety (pitch, pause, and pace) and body movements similar to that of an actor or actress on a stage	Low to moderate use of vocal variety and body language
Tend to be more formal	Tend to be less formal
May not employ the use of presentation software	In many cases uses presentation software
Typically does not involve direct audience interaction	Typically involves some form of direct audience interaction

Keep in mind that these differences are not hard-and-fast rules, so consider the list a representation of the general differences between the two.

THE SPEECH WRITING PROCESS

The second biggest obstacle speakers must overcome is not having a process for managing the entire speech development. People usually think that the hardest part of the speech is the delivery. But like a boxer, the fight is not won in the ring. It is won by the countless hours of preparation using a proven process leading up to the big moment. A good speech is no different. It is delivered after through preparation and following a proven process to achieve your ultimate goal. We're going to break this process down into two major parts: the speech *invitation* process and the speech *preparation* process. Let's get started.

Part 1: The Invitation Process

Congratulations! You've been invited or told (or better yet, hired) to deliver a speech. Now what? Where do you begin? That's the first hurdle you must overcome. Thankfully, you've got us as coaches to guide you through the first major aspect of your speech development process. It begins with the speech invitation intake process. During this step, there are several questions you'll want to answer to prepare for your speech. The easiest way to get these answers is to complete a pre-event questionnaire.

Pre-Event Questionnaire: 20 Questions to Answer to Deliver a Great Speech

Whether you interview the event planner or have him or her complete a form, this list of questions is vital to getting you started on the right path to a great speech delivery:

1. What's the title or theme of the event?

2. What's the date and time of my speech?

3. What's the length of time for my speech?

4. What's the address of the venue (street, city, state)?

5. What other topics are being presented during the event?

6. What are the three most important objectives for my presentation?

7. What would make my presentation a success for your audience?

8. Are there any sensitive issues or topics I should avoid?

9. What have you liked most about speakers you've had in the past?

10. What have you least enjoyed about speakers you've had in the past?

11. What will be the attire for attendees at this event? (Remember, presenters want to always take it a notch up.)

12. What's the estimated number of attendees?

13. Are there any aspects about the audience that are important for me to know (such as percentage of managers vs. nonmanagers in the audience, audience interests, etc.)?

14. What are the names and titles of your top leadership who will be attending the event?

15. Is there any industry jargon or terminology I should be familiar with, recognize, and/or use (or avoid)?

16. How would you describe your organization's culture?

17. What are the top three challenges your organization or group is currently facing?

18. Who are your primary competitors?

19. What areas or regions does your organization or group serve?

20. What delivery format (in-person, virtual only, or hybrid) will be used for the event?

The time and effort invested in obtaining these answers is well worth it. As one of our clients put it, "If you don't ask these questions, you'll waste a lot of time focusing on the administrative side of the presentation as opposed to focusing on the speech itself." Edit this list to fit your needs, but know that having a list to guide you in getting the information as efficiently as possible is essential. Armed with this data, you move on to the speech preparation process.

Part 2: The Preparation Process

Sun Tzu, author of *The Art of War*, famously said, "Every battle is won before it is fought." The same is true for great speech delivery. It comes down to what happens before you step in front of your audience. So, let's walk through the seven steps required to prepare for your speech.

Step 1: Establish Your Big Idea

To captivate your audience and deliver a powerful message, your Big Idea Statement must be clear. As discussed in Chapter 2, the Big Idea Statement identifies what's at stake for the audience. This sets the stage for you to spend the remainder of your speech building a case for the audience to take action.

Simon Sinek skyrocketed into the global speaking spotlight when he introduced the "start with why" concept during his "How Great Leaders Inspire Action" Puget Sound TEDx speech. His Big Idea was straightforward—great leaders inspire action by asking the question, "Why?" He opened his speech by asking "why" three times.

> Why is Apple so innovative? Year after year, after year, they're more innovative than all their competition. And yet, they're just a computer company. They have the same access to the same talent, the same agencies. . . . Why is it that Dr. Martin Luther King [Jr.] led the civil rights movement? He wasn't the only man who suffered in pre-civil

rights America. . . . And why is it that the Wright brothers were able to figure out controlled, powered man flight
when there were certainly other teams who were better
qualified, better funded?[1]

Simon asked these three "why" questions in the first few minutes of
his speech and then went on to say his discovery is "probably the world's
simplest idea." Simon's TEDx talk is a brilliant example of establishing
the purpose—the Big Idea Statement—at the very beginning of a speech.
Be sure your Big Idea is clear, and state it very early in your speech.

Step 2: Build the Case for Action

Now that you know your Big Idea, it's time to sell yourself and your
ideas. To do that effectively, you have to make the case for the audience. This is where what's known as proof points come into play. Proof
points are examples (the "proof") that what you're saying is true. In a
speech, these are usually shared via at least three stories that reinforce
your Big Idea. The most important aspect of building the case for action lies in finding examples that evoke an emotion in your audience
as you tell each story. (We'll delve into the nuances of how to use body
language and other techniques to tell the stories later in this chapter.)

Simon began to make the case for his "start with why" concept
by telling a story about Apple. He dropped his first memorable quote,
"People don't buy what you do, people buy why you do it." There's one
of the secrets to telling a memorable story in a speech. To make your
story memorable, say a memorable catchphrase or one-liner. You can
put the memorable quote on a slide to ensure you don't forget to say
it. If you want to get the maximum effect of the aha moment, say the
quote from memory. Your audience will be hooked and actively listening for your next story.

Simon's second story was an intriguing recount of the Wright brothers' triumph in winning the race into the skies. He proceeded to tell several other stories before ending with one about Dr. King. Stories made up the bulk of his persuasive speech, and it helped Simon make his case for *Start with Why*, which was also the title of his book. His book was a huge hit as a result of his TEDx speech.

Step 3: Be Aware of Your Movement

If you're new to presenting or it's something that scares you, we recommend being aware of your movement. Most people are unaware of the things they do when standing before a crowd. And those things, some of which are listed next, are very distracting and should be avoided:

- **Pacing.** Often the result of nervousness, people will begin to walk aimlessly around the stage.

- **Standing in one place.** Conversely, standing in one place with no natural movement should be avoided.

- **Flapping arms.** If you tend to speak with a lot of gestures, your arms and hands can become wildly distracting.

- **Self-massaging.** Another indication of nervousness is touching your face, rubbing your hands, moving your hair, and more.

To help reduce these distracting movements, follow a purposeful movement plan (PMP). A PMP consists of two parts—moving on stage and moving your body.

Moving on Stage

Think of a stage as being cut into three sections—the left side, middle, and right side. Practice casually walking from one section to the next and as you reach each section, stop walking. It's like doing a runway walk that models do when modeling clothing. They walk. Stop. Turn. And walk. By building the habit of walking to a section of the stage and stopping, you anchor yourself. Make your points and move to another section on purpose. Simply repeat the process. This ensures you are looking at each section of your audience and not favoring one side of the stage.

Moving Your Body

Body movements are the biggest habit challenge to overcome because these tend to be fairly ingrained. Rather than trying to eliminate these habits, we coach presenters to replace them with new habits, focusing specifically on hand usage and eye contact.

If you tend to keep your hands by your side, practice occasionally raising them up to emphasize a point. If you tend to talk with your hands, practice occasionally resting your arms and hands down by your side.

When it comes to eye contact, don't look into people's eyes, look just above their eyes at their foreheads. From a distance, you will appear to be looking at them when, in fact, you aren't.

Finally, to eliminate self-massaging, such as touching your face, rubbing your hands, etc., video your rehearsal to identify what triggers you to do any such behavior. Once you know the triggers, identify and practice a replacement habit to eliminate the bad one. For example, for people who habitually touch their faces, we help them identify a comfortable resting position for their arms and hands so that when they notice their hands coming up toward their faces, they learn to smoothly return them to a resting position. With enough practice, they stop bringing their hands up to their faces.

Take the time to identify what you're doing with your hands and replace bad habits with good ones.

Step 4: Plan Your Timing

There are four parts in a speech that require a timing strategy: the beginning, the transitions, the close, and the optional question and answer. Think through these questions as you plan your speech to ensure everything goes smoothly and none of these four sections are too short or too long:

- **The beginning.** How long will your opening be? From a stage perspective, where will you start and where will you need to be when it is time to make your transition into your first main point? Answering these questions establishes the plan for introducing you and your Big Idea to the audience.

- **The transitions.** What will trigger you to transition from one point to another? Will it be a memorable quote just as Simon shared his memorable one-liners at specific times? Will it be a story? Will it be a pause or provocative question? The timings used during the transitions are particularly important as they are the key ingredient for a smooth presentation delivery,

- **The close.** Where should you be on stage as you begin to close your speech? How much time will have elapsed before you begin your close? Will your pace of your speaking increase or decrease as you close the speech? With these answers, you can deliver a climactic close with precision.

- **The question and answer.** The Q&A is optional after a speech, but if you take questions, how long will the period last? Will you be responsible for selecting the individuals who ask questions, or will a moderator handle that? Thinking these questions through will keep your focus on adding value to your audience.

• • •

Mastering your timing requires practice, so rehearse each of these parts of your speech as much as possible and the result will be a very polished speech.

Step 5: Decide on Audience Engagement Tactics

The days of delivering a speech without any form of interaction are over. Audiences expect to be engaged, and we encourage you to purposefully plan ways to interact with them. So how will you engage your audience? As mentioned in previous chapters, you can ask provocative questions or conduct a survey or a poll. During a speech, another option is to come off the stage and interact directly with the audience. Mel Robbins, author of the bestseller *The 5 Second Rule* and one of the most-booked speakers in the world, loves doing this. Sardék does, too! But, it is not for everyone. Find what *is* for you and do it. We have one client who dances her way into the ballroom with lively music and then walks up the stairs to the stage to begin her speech. This can be tricky because it requires extreme breath control so that you're not huffing and puffing once you get to the mic. But done correctly, it has a *Wow* factor!

For speeches delivered virtually, consistently use the virtual platform tools and features to engage the audience. Ask a question and have the audience respond in the chat function. Have the audience use the emoticons as responses to your statements and queries. For training sessions, assign participants to small groups and place them in breakout rooms to complete various interactive activities such as:

- Case study reviews
- Group projects
- Training games

- Presentation teach-backs

- Team competitions

The more frequently you engage your virtual training participants, the better. The general rule of thumb for virtual training is to engage the participants every four to six minutes by prompting them to respond or do something. By repeatedly prompting the attendees to respond using the virtual platform's tools and features combined with the interactive activities listed previously, you can engage your participants once every six minutes with ease. Whether you're delivering a speech in-person, virtually, or both (hybrid), remember that people expect to be engaged, so design your speech to be engaging by using the tips and techniques in this chapter and Chapter 4.

Step 6: Practice Pitch, Pause, Pace, and Repetition
One area where speeches and presentations are noticeably different is the use of pitch, pause, pace, and repetition. The effectiveness of a speech relies heavily of their use whereas most presentations do not. Developing the skills and timing required to vary your vocal variety in a speech generally requires coaching and training, however you can learn the basics of when to use the techniques yourself, too.

Pitch
Pitch is the highness or lowness of your voice, not to be confused with the volume of your voice. In a speech, a speaker expresses emotion by changing voice pitch. For example, use a higher pitch to convey excitement and a lower pitch to convey seriousness. In general, change your pitch to match the emotions you wish to express. Unless you're very skilled at it, don't overuse pitch as that can make you appear fake.

Generally, vary your pitch wherever you wish to show an outward expression of emotion.

Pause

Pauses are the most underused tool in a speaker's toolkit because most people continuously talk from topic to topic without stopping. This is problematic in a speech because talking continuously does not provide the audience time to process what has been said.

Pauses are like stop signs. They force you to stop talking. When used properly, they are an incredibly powerful tool in your arsenal because they are attention-grabbers. What happens when someone stops talking? Listeners suddenly pay attention because the pattern of continuous sound has been interrupted and listeners need to know why. So, when should you pause? Pause whenever you wish to emphasize something during a speech. Use a pause to:

- Highlight a key point

- Create tension (This is especially true in Western countries as audiences from these countries tend to be uncomfortable with periods of silence.)

- Amplify an emotion

- Transition to the next subject

- Allow the audience time to process what you've just said

If you don't already have a habit of pausing when talking, you'll probably need to practice to use pauses effectively. The easiest way to learn how to use them is to . . . well, just use them. That was a pause in written language. See how it captured your attention? Use pauses. They are instant attention-grabbers.

Pace

Pace refers to the rate at which you speak. The average rate for English speakers in the United States is 150 words per minute. Conversational speech generally runs between 120 to 180 words per minute, so speaking less than 120 words is considered slow and speaking more than 180 words is fast.[2] The rate of speaking is heavily influenced by factors that include the speaker's culture, language, geographic location, and personality. The key is to speak so people can comfortably absorb what you are saying and vary your pace to add vocal variety to your speech to match the message you're sharing. So, when should you change your pace?

- Speed up to convey passion, urgency, or excitement

- Slow down to convey sadness, uncertainty, or fear

If you watch Simon Sinek's TEDx talk, "How Great Leaders Inspire Action," he spoke about 170 words per minute. And yet he varied his pace throughout, speeding up and slowing down to emphasize various points. Other TED speakers that we mention in this book such as Brené Brown and Sir Ken Robinson spoke in the 150–170 words per minute range. They also varied their pace quite consistently throughout their speeches. As you map out the key points of your speech, plan to vary your pace so it reinforces the message you want to send.

Repetition

Repeating a key word, phrase, or concept is a very effective way to help audiences remember what you said. In fact, you are bombarded by marketers who use repetition to burn their catchphrases and taglines into your memory. This is where the real power of the memorable catchphrase and one-liners comes into play. If you want the audience to remember your Big Idea, say it in a memorable one-liner and repeat it at least three times during your speech. People remember what is repeated. So, repeating a key phrase, main point, or tagline is a winning approach for making your message memorable.

Step 7: Know Your Body Language Cues

According to communication expert and author Vanessa Van Edwards, it's not enough to have great ideas, you also need to know how to communicate them. In her book *Cues: Master the Secret Language of Charismatic Communication*, she explains the reason some people are considered charismatic and the reason some messages go viral can be traced back to cues—the tiny signals we send when communicating.[3]

For some, body language cues can be a blind spot. There are four body language cues we encourage you to practice using because they can be the difference between an average and an exceptional speech:

- **The thumb pinch** (also known as the OK sign). Using your dominant hand, make an "OK" sign by pinching your thumb and index finger together. This is a great hand gesture to use when making a key point in your speech. (Be sure to be culturally mindful when using nonverbal signals, because in different cultures, some gestures may be considered offensive.)

- **Steepling.** Place your two hands together, palms touching, at chest level in front of you. This is known as steepling. It is also used by speakers when making a point or emphasizing an important concept.

- **Open palms.** Take your hands and act as if you are holding an invisible bowl that is about 12"–18" in diameter at chest level. This is known as open palms, and it is used when the speaker wants to convey openness or acceptance as a point of emphasis.

- **Smile while talking.** While this might seem easy, doing it is a bit harder than you think. Smiling while talking is a powerful way to engage your audience, so definitely practice doing this naturally before a speech. Charismatic speakers smile while talking when they want to get the audience's buy-in and when they want their speeches to evoke joy and pleasure.

To see examples of the body language cues in use, watch videos of the well-known and celebrity speakers such as John Maxwell, Les Brown, President Ronald Regan, President Barack Obama, and Simon T. Bailey. Use these easy-to-adopt tips and techniques, and you're well on your way to delivering an enjoyable, entertaining, and memorable speech.

Let's summarize what you've learned. You now know the difference between a speech and a presentation. The pre-event questionnaire will enable you to collect important information during the speech invitation process. And finally, use the seven-step speech preparation process to create a highly memorable speech.

The Speech Preparation Process

Step 1: Establish Your Big Idea

Step 2: Build the Case for Action

Step 3: Be Aware of Your Movement

Step 4: Plan Your Timing

Step 5: Decide on Audience Engagement Tactics

Step 6: Practice Pitch, Pause, Pace, and Repetition

Step 7: Know Your Body Language Cues

ESSENTIAL TAKEAWAYS

- Practice makes proficient when presenting a speech.
- Use pre-event questions to help you prepare and deliver a great speech.
- Always know your purpose and build your case for action.
- Follow these best practices for delivering your speech: use purposeful movement; get your timing down; engage your audience; mind your pitch, pause, pace, and repetition; and practice appropriate body language cues.

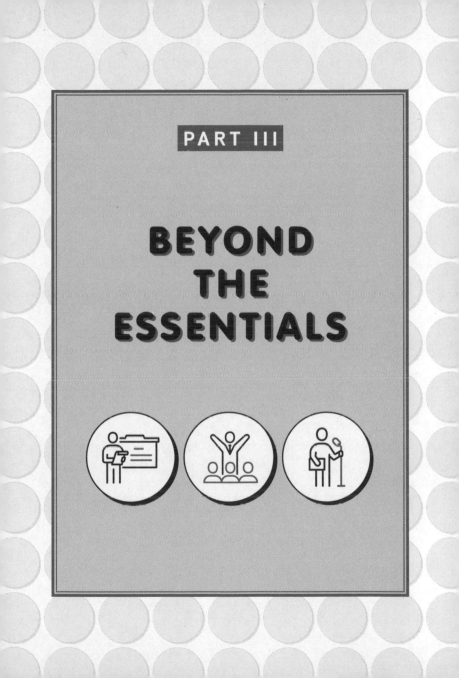

PART III

BEYOND
THE
ESSENTIALS

Delivering Presentations
for a Living

If you're comfortable speaking in public and believe you're ready to up your game and take that next step to make this a career, we applaud you! Presenting professionally is a fun, fulfilling way to make a living. If you like traveling, meeting new people, and experiencing new environments, this might be the right fit for you. You'll experience cultures and cuisines far from your own and meet interesting and lovely people all along the way.

This is a career where enthusiasm, fortitude, and tenacity are the triad of success. It's also a career that has as many twists and turns as any Colorado mountain switchback. It's a very competitive field, and you must remain dedicated to marketing yourself to stay relevant, current, and visible while also being fully committed to hard, physical days on the road and unwavering commitment in unsteady economic times. Long stretches away from home can leave you missing both your family and your cozy bed. But through it all, we've thoroughly enjoyed the ups and downs of our careers, and we think you will too.

That being said, while there are a lot of fun perks, it's also a competitive career and business, and it needs to be treated as such. Profitability should be your goal, not seeing the Egyptian Pyramids or the Golden Gate Bridge.

You've got to know your margins of profitability, which includes what you take home financially after your speaking engagement. You also have to consider your overhead, such as taxes (what's your bracket?). You'll need to think about how much you'll pay—and other fees associated with being self-employed that you'll be responsible for, such as independent health insurance. Other costs include a speaker bureau commission or talent manager fees. There may be other speaker management fees as well, such as research materials, required technical equipment, wardrobe, office help, supplies, and more. Be sure to take each of these into consideration as you think through whether speaking is the right career for you.

KEYS TO BUILDING A SUCCESSFUL LIVING AS A PROFESSIONAL PRESENTER

Many people want to get paid to present for a living but don't know exactly how to do it. There is a lack of understanding about what it takes to get hired, brand and market services, and overcome barriers to generate revenue as a speaker, trainer, author, consultant, or coach. It is entirely possible to build a successful, lucrative career as a presenter—we and many others are living proof. In the following sections, we discuss the foundations that have helped us launch and maintain careers as professional presenters.

Advertise Your *Wow* Factor

Success as a professional speaker begins by answering two questions: What's your *Wow* factor? How are you going to prove it?

At its most basic, your *Wow* factor is that special something that gets you noticed—your sparkle or sizzle. It's what sets you apart from the crowd. Your *Wow* factor is a multifaceted concept that combines your personal attributes like self-confidence and emotional intelligence, along with behavioral attributes like how you carry yourself in front of others, plus the signature style with which you deliver your presentation. Your *Wow* factor is how you articulate what makes you different, compelling, and undeniably worth hiring for the next big event, book deal, or consulting gig. It is the best parts of your personality amplified and projected across the room; it's vital to sell your product.

So, how do you prove your *Wow* factor? When you've got it on the inside, you should show it on the outside through branding yourself as *the* source for your subject. Use your website to market your services. For professional speakers, posting videos on your social media platforms enables you to promote your message, showcase your work, maintain visibility, and show potential decision makers your *Wow* in action.

Be Known for Solving a Single Problem

When Sardék launched his business in 2007, he was promoting more than 36 different training courses. He consistently sold two and that frustrated him. He struggled to understand why, and with the help of a business coach, the answer became obvious. Sardék was well-known for training trainers how to be incredibly engaging. If you've ever seen him in action, you understand why.

With his understanding of his *Wow* factor, he launched his signature program, "Facilitating with Impact!," at the Association for Talent Development (ATD) annual conference in 2011. An obsessive focus on his signature program fueled Sardék's rise on a global scale. In 2018, ATD named Sardék as a top 25 global thought leader in talent development. That credibility was what he needed to take off. And, it all started with being known for solving a single problem and creating a signature-branded program.

The most fascinating thing begins to happen when you become known for something. It's called being a subject matter expert (SME), and the results of being known as a SME are astonishing. Your clients are confident in your work and feel they can really trust you. As a result, client testimonials and referrals become a norm, and then over time, your clients start asking you to solve additional problems. Once this happens, you're set to begin diversifying your offerings into more training, coaching, and consulting products and services.

Presenters who do exactly that—begin with a narrow focus and become known for solving a single problem—are much more likely to scale their business practice at a faster pace than those who don't.

Know Your Customer Base

Once you know your *Wow* factor and what one problem you can solve better than anyone else, you can begin considering who needs the answers you have to give by clearly defining your ideal customer. In our experience, failing to do this is a fundamental mistake many people make, and it can often lead to long-term, catastrophic consequences for those who are serious about being a paid presenter.

For example, a person may have experience coaching leaders, so he or she starts a coaching business. A person with years training employees launches a training business. While that experience is invaluable and necessary to become a professional speaker, clearly defining who your ideal client is and what problems that client has is just as important, if not more. So where do you get started? We suggest setting your sights on the right groups, conferences, audiences, and paying customers. Yes, paying customers. If you're not paid, you are a volunteer and your presentations become a hobby, not a business. So, target those who have a budget to pay presenters for their time and expenses.

Here's how we suggest you start your investigation:

Read magazines, books, and periodicals in your subject area. Magazines, like *Success*, appeal to speaker bureaus. Dig deeper by going online to see what presenters are featured on their speaker bureau listing and follow and like their social media.

When you get a clearer picture of who their audience is, you may find you share the same market. If that's the case, you'll be able to learn a lot just from their daily posts and people's responses. You can also look at the readership of contributors in your space. What articles and contributions are timely and newsworthy? Apply these points to your own presentation.

Not sure where else to look? Search online for your subject matter and see who's known for specializing in it. Google "your topic + Speaker," "your topic + Conference," or "your topic + Author" to find speakers who cover a specific topic that may be like yours.

Join an association. Many professions have an association that hires speakers to deliver keynote presentations and lead breakout sessions on a wide variety of topics. For example, the Association for Talent Development (ATD), Society for Human Resource Management (SHRM), American Society of Association Executives (ASAE), and National Speakers Association (NSA) host annual conferences, and many have local chapter events that also feature opportunities for speaking. In addition, associations often have an international presence, which can open doors for you on a global scale.

Capitalize on word of mouth. Referrals are considered one of the best ways to get presentation opportunities. If you've presented somewhere and received positive feedback and/or audience ratings, ask the meeting planners or attendees for referrals and recommendations.

Tap into existing clients. Don't be a best-kept secret. Let your existing client base know that you're available to speak on your subject matter. They can't know you're available to present to their company or group if you don't tell them.

Reach out to colleges and universities. Colleges and universities are constantly seeking to expose their students and alumni to experts like you. Start by contacting continuing education departments, specific online or on-campus programs seeking speakers, campus activities, clubs, and so on.

Explore hotels and convention center websites. Get familiar with the hotels and convention centers in popular conference destination cities, like Las Vegas, Orlando, and San Diego. Their websites show upcoming events that you can use as potential targets for future speaking opportunities. If you identify a conference that could be a fit for you, search for the event planner or meeting planner associated with that event and contact the planner to express your interest in being a speaker at the next or future events.

Introduce yourself to meeting planners (or meeting professionals) and speaker bureaus. Websites for meeting professionals often showcase planners who are seeking to connect with presenters. For example, Meeting Professionals International (MPI) has a chapter in almost every large city where you can attend a local chapter meeting to introduce yourself and look for contacts.

Look at speaker bureau websites, such as Washington Speakers Bureau or Eagles Talent. These offer a wealth of information on speaker fee ranges, requirements, popular topics, and more. Research who they are marketing and in what categories. Be aware that to be considered by any bureau or meeting planner, you'll need a speaker website, sizzle reel or presentation video, and engaging social media presence with a significant followership.

Join your local chamber of commerce. Chambers are represented locally and statewide and have strong relationships with local businesses and influential leaders. Tap into this source for new contacts and opportunities. This kind of networking is golden, but it requires time, membership, and relationship-building.

Listen to podcasts. Identify the influencers of your ideal target market and subscribe to their podcasts. Often, guests share where they will be speaking.

Develop a Positioning Strategy

Cindy Huggett is known as the guru on virtual training. Jack and Patti Phillips are known as the aces of defining return on investment for training programs. John Chen is known as the expert on building teams using technology and gamification. The successful businesses these individuals run are not accidents. Like all highly successful professional presenters, they use marketing and a brand positioning strategy to define where they fit in the marketplace.

Since you've now established your audience, know what you want to sell, and are showing off your *Wow* factor whenever you can, it's time to get your own strategy in place. To do this properly, your digital assets—website, content marketing, social media campaigns, reputation, etc.—must have a consistent message that attracts your ideal customers. Unless you possess the skills to develop a positioning strategy, enlisting the help of a coach or consultant is a smart business decision. Never consider the cost of a coach or consultant an expense (until you do your taxes, that is). Consider it an investment because that's what it is.

Business statistics across the globe indicate that professional presenters thrive with the help of outstanding mentors, executive coaching, consultants from their industry, and resources widely available on the internet. So, knowing the difference between cost and an investment can mean the difference between $100 and $1 million on your balance sheet.

Part of this strategy should also be building your contacts, which includes your email list, because as Tony Robbins says, "If you don't have an email list, you don't have a business." You want to continuously grow your list of prospects and then contact them in order to build a sustainable scalable business. A customer relationship management (CRM) system and an email marketing tool will help get this done. There are many on the market, and several CRMs have email marketing capabilities built in. Ask around and get other people's advice and input.

There are no shortcuts around this requirement. Hope is not a strategy.

Establish a Solid Social Media Presence

To succeed as a professional presenter, it's now necessary to have a solid social media base for visibility. And this part of the job requires consistency, strong messaging, and devoted time for quality posting. The good news is, unless you're engaged in paid advertising online, social media exposure is free. Depending on your originality and ability to produce quality content, there is no limit to what you can do or gain as a return on your investment.

If you don't have a social media account, it's time to launch one. Start by researching what channels your ideal customers use most frequently and target your efforts to post there for maximum reach. You'll want to use consistent branding across all channels so it is easy for people to find you.

In terms of posting, depending on which platform you're using, you may post several times a day. You can also post reels and stories, which we suggest you do two to three times a week. When posting content, remember your main goal in presenting is to solve a challenge by informing, instructing, persuading, or entertaining—focus your content on providing those answers. Social media provides a time-sensitive window to every event and presentation happening, so plan your content ahead of time while also leaving room for flexibility for breaking news.

Social media is great for connecting with your audience, but it's also a great way to learn about upcoming opportunities that relate to your brand, such as conferences and events. Search hashtags like #eventprofs, #NSA, #meetingplanners, #leadershipconferences, #key notespeakers, and #conference to see what's happening in fields related to you and contact event planners and bureaus to express your interest. Popular platforms like LinkedIn, TikTok, Instagram, and others showcase presentation opportunities.

When people ask Anne how she measures the results of her social media, her reply is analytics, but more importantly, focusing on the quality leads she gets. For that reason, don't focus on likes and followers as much as quality leads, including people who direct message (DM) you for more information, send you emails to request more info to buy your services, or eventually sign on with you for speaking, executive coaching, or consulting services you provide.

Build Something Bigger on Social Media

Anne lives at the beach in Southern California, making the weather and the Pacific Ocean a beautiful backdrop. One day while walking her dog Cloud, it dawned on her that she wasn't fully using her environment to sell her speaker practice, her books, and her talent management business. That day #30SecondsAtTheBeach was born. Now approaching its fifth year in production, Anne used her media experience (formerly a TV producer and talk show host who now writes for the entertainment industry in Los Angeles) to produce a daily video series called *30 Seconds at the Beach*. The series took off like a rocket. She keeps her message to 30 seconds and filming at the beach became the winning formula that transformed her social media strategy into revenues, book sales, and exciting new clients worldwide. Her messages are reliably consistent and inspiring, just like her books and speeches. Her followers know exactly what to expect.

This series also expanded into another series called *A Day in the Life of an Author*, which focuses on tips and tools for writers. It, too, is filmed at the beach or at a local harbor nearby and has gained significant popularity and lots of new clients.

You, too, can create a social media series. In television this is referred to as creating a franchise for an existing body of work—and you can do this using this framework:

- **Select a theme.** Choose a theme you feel comfortable presenting about and a corresponding visual, both of which should be related to your brand. Anne, for example, uses her locale at the beach as her theme backdrop for her social media.

- **Be consistent.** You'll build a loyal audience and true connections by *consistently* posting content that adds value to them. Whether you share content daily or a few days a week, pick a schedule and stick with it.

- **Stay on message.** While you can mix up your content by posting about current events or holidays, always find a way to connect back to your brand.

- **Add value fast.** Condense your posts into bite-sized facts, tips, or tools that fit into the format of the social media platform you're posting on.

Conduct a Competitive Analysis to Set Your Price

One of the most challenging aspects of delivering presentations for a living is determining how much to charge for your services. This will largely depend on your business model and reputation, and conducting a competitive analysis is the best way to get started. Look at what your competitors are charging to get an idea of the ballpark you're competing in. Keep in mind location is important here. If you're working in New York, San Francisco, or London, your fees will reflect what the market can bear, plus cost of living.

Professional associations and LinkedIn groups are great for researching pricing trends. You should also tap into your professional networks.

One important tip to keep in mind when negotiating your price with a prospective client is to keep the focus of the conversation on value as opposed to price. This helps you avoid being taken advantage of. Be confident in the value you offer, and you'll rarely have seller's remorse.

THE IMPORTANCE OF HAVING A SUPPORT SYSTEM

Before wrapping up this chapter, let's talk about the importance of prioritizing the people you love. Being on the road to promote your work can be an incredibly rewarding experience, but it can also take a toll on your relationships—if you let it, that is. The most fulfilled and successful speakers we know go the extra mile to make sure they stay connected to their support networks while they're on the road. This can be difficult when you're physically exhausted or are in a different time zone, but it's nonetheless vital to your mental health while you're away.

If you have young children, care for elderly parents, or have a family structure that cannot accommodate your long absences, a career in professional presenting may prove a difficult work-life balance for you. We recommend having a heart-to-heart conversation with your support network to determine if launching this kind of career is the right fit for your family at the right time.

• • •

We've weathered the ups and downs of this sometimes volatile industry to find success in our careers as professional presenters. If you decide to take the same career path—and we hope that you do—be sure to crunch your numbers, do your homework, shore up your support systems, and buckle in for an exciting ride! We look forward to seeing you on the circuit.

ESSENTIAL TAKEAWAYS

- Professional speaking, training, consulting, and coaching is a flexible, rewarding, fun yet competitive and volatile career.

- It's a business and must be treated as such; it's about profitability.

- Successful professional presenters know and market their *Wow* factor.

- Clearly define your ideal customers, and adopt a system for managing customer relationships and attracting, nurturing, and converting leads into customers.

The Ongoing Journey of Presenting

Throughout our long and varied careers, each time we've gotten in front of an audience, we've felt the electricity of being in the spotlight. That's part of the reason we've chosen this career. Even if you're not a professional speaker—if you're called to speak in front of a group or you have vital information to share—being the messenger is a gift.

Your audience is an untapped resource of simmering energy and it's up to you to tap into it. You're the spark that will ignite their inner fire to act on your message, and you have the ability to inform, instruct/ educate, persuade, and entertain when all eyes are on you. That is both a great privilege and a great responsibility, so become as good at this as you possibly can and never forget it's never about you, it's always about them.

Speaking of them, when you're in front of an audience, constantly remember that you're establishing a relationship with them. Throughout this book you've learned you must be authentic, relatable, and believable for them to pick up what you're putting down. These elements are key, and knowing your reasons for being a presenter will ultimately help you establish a rapport with your audience. In the self-assessment at the beginning of Part II, you dug a little deeper into your "whys" of doing what you're doing. Maybe you're drawn to being in the spotlight, maybe your job requires it, or maybe your message is vital to the future of humankind. But whatever your reasons, the fact remains that your authenticity is vital to your delivery and how your audience responds to you.

Once you've solidified and internalized your reasons, the "hows" of what you're doing will fall into place. That's where the skills we've outlined will come into play to help you practice your craft. In thinking about how you structure your presentation, you've learned that your story must have a beginning, middle, and end. You may even find it helpful to visualize what you want your audience to feel at the end of your speech and build your presentation from that angle. Your message, accompanied by compelling visuals and delivered with powerful yet memorable stories, has the potential to be remembered or acted upon. It's your delivery that makes your story unique.

Whether your signature style launches by cracking a joke, citing a statistic, or telling a brief story, it's how you grab your audience's attention and get your message across. You captivate the room by delivering your information that gets the audience right in the heart and the head. Your style will help make your stories memorable to your audience, and that is the whole point.

You want your audience to leave the room on a higher emotional plane than when they entered—informed, entertained, persuaded, or instructed. With a clever and imaginative opener, you'll grab their attention and hold their interest. Once you've got that, continue delivering your message, emphasizing your main points along the way. And when it's time to wrap up, you've learned an energetic and compelling close makes your presentation memorable and actionable.

The reasons that compelled you to read this book led you this far. Regardless of why you give a presentation or the subjects on which you speak, getting on stage or in front of a room full of people to deliver a message is your main goal. How you do that is solely up to you. Whenever eyes are on you, remember to keep calm and carry on. You've learned that there is no perfect, but practice makes proficient! By practicing your craft, you'll hone your presentation skills until they are second nature to you. And when you're ready to take your presentation skills to the next level, you have an idea of how pros like coaches, authors, trainers, and consultants pull it off. Your confidence will grow each time you step in front of a different group; you'll feel the electricity and use it to power you through to the end.

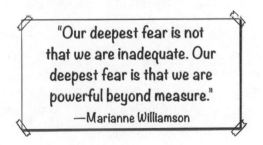

"Our deepest fear is not that we are inadequate. Our deepest fear is that we are powerful beyond measure."
—Marianne Williamson

Presentation Essentials Toolkit

To support your development as a presenter, we wanted to provide you with this at-a-glance toolkit, which includes:

- The Dos and Don'ts of Presenting

- Presentation Structure Guidelines

- Presentation Development Worksheet

- Postpresentation Evaluation—Speedback Coaching on the Spot

- High-Impact Storytelling Worksheet

- Top Resources for Smart Presenters

THE DOS AND DON'TS OF PRESENTING

Dos

- Be appropriately energetic and engaging.
- Use an attention-grabbing opener.
- Step from behind the podium.
- Use audience-appropriate language.
- Use appealing visuals and easy-to-read fonts.
- Know the essence of your Big Idea.
- Use physical movement to emphasize your message.
- Be authentic.
- Use catchphrases and one-liners to make your message memorable.
- Close your presentation with an unforgettable call to action.
- Think on the fly.
- Mention you're available after your presentation for a meet and greet.
- Make powerful pauses.

Don'ts

- Be repetitive, boring, or monotone.

- Stumble on your words or ask if the mic is working.

- Lean on or hide behind the podium.

- Swear.

- Use bad graphics or too much text in your visuals.

- Read directly from your notes.

- Wring your hands, touch your hair or face, or tuck your hands behind your head.

- Be fake.

- Ramble on with too much information.

- Say "thank you" and close your presentation.

- Make up statistics or figures on the fly.

- Sell from the stage or be a know-it-all

- Say "um" or "ah," or "uh" repeatedly.

PRESENTATION STRUCTURE GUIDELINES

In Chapter 2, we shared guidelines for creating an effective presentation. This at-a-glance list provides that framework for you with just the basics to help you with your next presentation:

Pillar 1: The Situation

The presenter defines the problem being addressed, creates a Big Idea Statement to motivate the audience to take action after the presentation, and identifies what's at stake if the audience fails to take action.

- **Part 1: Identify the problems your audience faces.**

  - Are the problems urgent, widespread, or expensive?

  - Rank the severity of each problem.

  - Choose the most severe problem to address.

- **Part 2: Add your expert insights for overcoming the problem.**

  - Create "aha" moments or Moments of Truth that confront what the audience believes to be true.

- **Part 3: Detail the stakes involved.**

  - Define what's at risk if the audience fails to act.

Pillar 2: Building the Case for Change

This is where the presenter builds the case for change by making one to three key points that challenge the status quo.

- Expose the audience struggle.

- Identify the conflict.

- Reiterate how your Big Idea Statement solves the audience problems.

Pillar 3: The Better Future and Call to Action

This is where the presenter defines a better future and appeals for a call to action.

- Recap the stakes if your audience fails to act.

- Specify the actions you want the audience to take.

- Invite your audience to take specific action.

PRESENTATION DEVELOPMENT WORKSHEET

Use this helpful worksheet when planning your presentation. Fill in the blanks appropriate to your content.

Pillar 1: The Situation	
Part 1: Identify the Problems Your Audience Faces	
Are the problems urgent? If so, identify why.	Problem 1: Problem 2: Problem 3:
Are the problems widespread? If so, identify why.	Problem 1: Problem 2: Problem 3:
Are the problems expensive? If so, identify why.	Problem 1: Problem 2: Problem 3:
Rank the severity of each problem on a scale of 1 to 5, with 1 being low and 5 being high.	Problem 1 rank: Problem 2 rank: Problem 3 rank:
Choose the most highly ranked (and thereby the most severe) problem to address and write it here.	Most severe problem:

Part 2: Add Your Expert Insights for Overcoming the Most Severe Problem	
Create "aha" moments or Moments of Truth that confront what the audience believes to be true.	Aha moment #1 addressing Problem #1 Aha moment #2 addressing Problem #1 Aha moment #3 addressing Problem #1
Part 3: Detail the Stakes Involved	
What are the stakes?	Stake #1 Stake #2 Stake #3
Define what's at risk if the audience fails to act.	Risk #1 Risk #2 Risk #3

Pillar 2: Building the Case for Change

Build your case for change by making one to three key points that challenge the status quo.

Expose the audience struggle.	
Identify the conflict.	
Reiterate how your Big Idea Statement solves the audience problem.	

Pillar 3: The Better Future and Call to Action	
Recap the stakes if your audience fails to act.	Stake #1 Stake #2 Stake #3
Specify the actions you want the audience to take.	
Invite your audience to take specific action.	

POSTPRESENTATION EVALUATION— SPEEDBACK COACHING ON THE SPOT

Every reputable presentation should have a mechanism for audience feedback that's fast and accurate. We like to call this "speedback coaching." How else will you know if you're hitting the mark with your audience unless you receive feedback? Or how will you know if you're improving, for that matter? With this in mind, we've provided a sample evaluation form you can use or adapt to measure your presentations.

How to Use the Postpresentation Evaluation

If you're evaluating your own presentation, we recommend taking a video with a smartphone or camera of yourself presenting. Try to keep your trial run short, about three minutes or so. Play the video and use the evaluation to critique yourself, making notes on where you can improve and where you already shine. Remember, in areas where you feel strong, focus on how you can amplify them and let those strengths work for you.

When to Use the Postpresentation Evaluation

Presenters often distribute evaluations to receive feedback from their audiences because an evaluation is a great tool for continuous growth. It's not a way to embarrass presenters or make them feel inadequate; on the contrary, presenters should seek out feedback in order to refine their craft. We encourage you to adapt the evaluation in this section to share with your audience after your presentations.

How to Use the Postpresentation Evaluation in a Group

When you're learning how to present and you're trying to up your game, it's great to have reliable feedback and an audience you know. Many organizations have groups where you can practice presenting, and this evaluation can be perfect for those types of settings.

Make copies of the following evaluation, giving a copy to every audience member for each presenter. (Reminder: This is a time to be honest and helpful. Insults or negative comments are not allowed and can be deflating for everyone involved. Leave your comments in the spirit of providing helpful feedback.)

Give everyone three minutes to present their speech or specialized presentation. Assign a timekeeper in the audience and tell everyone they should be focused on the presenter during their time and should not be writing as they speak. There should be time set aside after each presenter for everyone to record their thoughts.

It's also a great idea to remind everyone that the entire evaluation does not have to be completed. Instead, focus on areas that will be of the most help to the presenter. If she or he spoke too softly, that's a great note to make. If they soared with confidence or told a heartfelt story that grabbed everyone's attention, make note of that as well.

The feedback a presenter receives from these evaluations can provide an enormous growth opportunity. Each presenter can study the comments and make notes on things that resonated with the audience or things that may have been confusing. And, remember, when you're the one completing this sheet on someone's presentation, be *supportive*, *helpful*, *specific*, *kind*, and *empathetic*.

Presenter's Name	
Presentation Topic/ Session Name	

On a scale from 1 (opportunity for improvement) to 10 (approaching excellence), please rank your presenter on the following categories:

1	2	3	4	5	6	7	8	9	10

Category	Ranking	Comments
The presenter delivered material in a clear, concise, and logical manner.		
The presenter used powerful storytelling and anecdotes.		
The presenter had knowledge and expertise on the subject matter.		
The presenter was able to grab and keep my interest and attention through eye contact, humor, gestures, movement, etc.		

Category	Ranking	Comments
The presenter was well-prepared.		
The presenter was energetic and enthusiastic.		
The presenter stayed within the timeframe parameters.		
The presenter spoke in a clear and articulate manner.		
The presenter engaged the audience.		
The presenter opened with an attention-grabbing story, anecdote, or phrase.		
The presenter used practical examples and useful techniques.		

Category	Ranking	Comments
The presenter used visual aids/videos/ music/learning tools appropriately and effectively.		
The presenter was well-rehearsed.		
The presenter had his or her own confident signature style.		
The presenter had quality pitch, tone, pace, volume, and clarity.		
The presenter used stunning images.		
The presenter had energy and lively gestures to punctuate points.		
The presenter moved around and was animated.		

Category	Ranking	Comments
The presenter used catchphrases or one-liners that people wrote down.		
The presenter used appropriate humor and gave us a mental break.		
The presenter was approachable and real, not phony.		
The presenter had structure: a compelling opener, rich content, and a memorable close.		
The presenter answered questions effectively.		
Additional comments:		

HIGH-IMPACT STORYTELLING WORKSHEET

Every story contains three characters: the Hero, the Villain, and the Guide. We created this High-Impact Storytelling Worksheet so you can easily craft and create stories (with these three characters in mind) to captivate your audience and make your message memorable. By using story structure, you:

- Eliminate irrelevant information

- Obliterate confusion

- Engage your audience

- Inspire action

Step 1: Identify the Hero

Define your main character and answer the question: "What does the Hero want?" In a presentation, your client/audience is the Hero.

Step 2: Define the Villain

The Villain represents the problem, challenge, or barrier preventing the Hero from getting what he or she wants.

Step 3: Expose the Conflict

How does the existence of the Villain make the Hero feel? That is the conflict. The conflict can also be between what the Hero wants and what the Hero believes to be true. The level of conflict the Hero experiences should increase as your story unfolds.

Step 4: Define the Moment of Truth

The Moment of Truth creates a point of no return for the Hero and makes inaction impossible. The Hero must act in order to have any chance of achieving the goal.

Step 5: Introduce the Guide

The Guide provides the Hero with the advice, support, or solution required for the Hero to achieve the goal. In your presentation, the presenter or the solution serves as the Guide.

Step 6: Take Action

The Hero uses the solution. In your presentation, this is a great place to share an example of a client using your solution to achieve the goal.

TOP RESOURCES FOR SMART PRESENTERS

This list of resources vital to presenters has and continues to evolve. During the course of our careers, we've found the following resources essential to sharpening and growing our presentation skills:

- Toastmasters International, the world-renowned nonprofit, has been teaching public speaking and leadership skills since 1924.

- Podcasts such as Toastmasters, The Speaker Lab, The Public Speaker's Quick and Dirty Tips for Improving Your Communication Skills, and many more.

- TED Talks and the TED Audio Collective (bonus here is you will learn about presenting and can watch other presenters' signature styles).

- The Association for Talent Development is the world's largest association for training professionals.

- The National Speakers Association is a leading resource for those who pursue a career as a professional speaker.

- YouTube.

- The Ethos3 blog, The Accidental Communicator, Speaking About Presenting, and any of the articles on quick and dirty tips when you do a Google search on "public speaking."

Notes

Chapter 2

1. Carmine Gallo, "What the Best Presenters Do Differently," *Harvard Business Review*, April 27, 2022.
2. John Maxwell Podcast, "Alan Mulally: Driving Ford Through Crisis," September 16, 2020, https://podcasts.apple.com/us/podcast/alan-mulally-driving-ford -through-crisis/id1416206538?i=1000491420491.

Chapter 3

1. James Clear, *Atomic Habits: An Easy & Proven Way to Build Good Habits & Break Bad Ones* (New York: Avery, 2018).
2. Ken Blanchard and Spencer Johnson, *The New One Minute Manager* (New York: William Morrow, 1982); Ken Blanchard and Claire Diaz-Ortiz, *One Minute Mentoring: How to Find and Work With a Mentor—And Why You'll Benefit from Being One* (New York: William Morrow, 2017); and Ken Blanchard, *Gung Ho! Turn On the People in Any Organization* (New York: William Morrow, 1998).
3. Tony Buzan and Barry Buzan, *The Mind Map Book: How to Use Radiant Thinking to Maximize Your Brain's Untapped Potential* (New York: PLUME/Penguin Books, 1996).

Chapter 4

1. Stephen R. Covey, A. Roger Merrill, and Rebecca R. Merrill, *First Things First* (New York: Free Press, 1996).
2. Nancy Duarte, *Resonate—Present Visual Stories That Transform Audiences* (Hoboken, NJ: John Wiley & Sons, 2010), xviii.
3. Merriam-Webster, s.v. "novel," https://www.merriam-webster.com/dictionary /novel.
4. Jack Canfield, *The Success Principles: How to Get from Where You Are to Where You Want to Be* (New York: HarperCollins, 2005), 131.

Chapter 5

1. Tamsen Webster, *Find Your Red Thread. Make Your Big Ideas Irresistible* (Vancouver, BC: Page Two Books, 2021), 13, 9.
2. Ibid, 95.

Chapter 6

1. Sir Ken Robinson, "Do schools kill creativity?" TED2006, https://www.ted.com/talks/sir_ken_robinson_do_schools_kill_creativity.
2. Jeffrey Gitomer, Quotefancy, https://quotefancy.com/quote/2278768/David-Nihill-The-end-of-laughter-is-followed-by-the-height-of-listening-Jeffrey-Gitomer.
3. MADD Statistics https://www.madd.org/statistics.
4. Aaron De Smet, Bonnie Dowling, Marino Mugayar, and Bill Schaninger, *Great Attrition or Great Attraction? The Choice Is Yours*, McKinsey and Company, September 8, 2021.
5. Leigh Branham, *The 7 Hidden Reasons Employees Leave: How to Recognize Subtle Signs Before It's Too Late* (New York: Amacom Books, 2005).
6. Marilee Adams, *Change Your Questions, Change Your Life* (Oakland, CA: Berrett-Koehler, 2016).
7. David Nihill, "23 Tips from Comedians to Be Funnier in Your Next Presentation (via the book *Do You Talk Funny?*)," SlideShare, December 21, 2015 , https://www.slideshare.net/daithin/23-tips-from-comedians-to-be-funnier-in-your-next-presentation.
8. Lea Growth, "These Are the Most Common Passwords—Do Yours Make the List?" Reader's Digest, May 18, 2022, https://www.rd.com/article/passwords-hackers-guess-first.
9. *We Choose to Go to the Moon*, Wikipedia, https://en.wikipedia.org/wiki/We_choose_to_go_to_the_Moon.

Chapter 7

1. Color Wheel, Canva, https://www.canva.com/colors/color-wheel/.
2. HubSpot, https://blog.hubspot.com/marketing/free-visual-content-creation-templates-li.

Chapter 8

1. Mark Forsyth, *The Elements of Eloquence* (New York: Berkley Books, 2014).

2. John Maxwell, John Maxwell Leadership Podcast, "How to Gain Influence—Part 1," February 9, 2022, https://johnmaxwellleadershippodcast.com/episodes/john-maxwell-how-to-gain-influence-1.

3. John Maxwell, John Maxwell Leadership Podcast, "Leader Vision—How to See More and See Before," August 22, 2018, https://johnmaxwellleadershippodcast.com/episodes/leadership-vision-how-to-see-more-and-see-before.

4. John Maxwell, John Maxwell Leadership Podcast, "Leader Vision—How to See and Sculpt the Future," November 17, 2021, https://johnmaxwellleadershippodcast.com/episodes/john-maxwell-leader-vision-how-to-see-and-sculpt-the-future.

5. John Maxwell, John Maxwell Team Podcast Series, "7.2: Who Are the Make a Difference People." (Original podcast was provided on tape to Sardék Love and is not available online.)

6. John Maxwell, John Maxwell Leadership Podcast, "How to Gain Influence—Part 1," February 9, 2022, https://johnmaxwellleadershippodcast.com/episodes/john-maxwell-how-to-gain-influence-1.

7. Craig Groeschel, Craig Groeschel Leadership Podcast, "75: Becoming a Leader Who Anticipates," February 9, 2022, https://www.life.church/leadershippodcast/becoming-a-leader-who-anticipates/.

8. Craig Groeschel, Craig Groeschel Leadership Podcast, "104: High Impact Habits for Successful Leaders", February 9, 2022, https://www.life.church/leadershippodcast/high-impact-habits-for-successful-leaders/.

9. Ibid.

10. Ibid.

11. James Clear, *Atomic Habits: An Easy & Proven Way to Build Good Habits & Break Bad Ones* (New York: Avery, 2018).

12. Simon Sinek, *Start with Why: How Great Leaders Inspire Everyone to Take Action* (New York: Portfolio/Penguin, 2009).

13. Kerry Patterson, Joseph Grenny, David Maxfield, Ron McMillan, and Al Switzler, *Influencer: The New Science of Leading Change*, 2nd ed. (New York: McGraw Hill, 2013).

14. John F. Kennedy, "President John F. Kennedy's Inaugural Address (1961)," National Archives, January 20, 1961, https://www.archives.gov/milestone-documents/president-john-f-kennedys-inaugural-address.

Chapter 9

1. Brené Brown, *The Price of Invulnerability*, TEDx KC, October 12, 2010, https:// youtu.be/_UoMXF73j0c.

2. Simon Sinek, *The Price of Invulnerability*, TEDx KC, October 12, 2010, https:// youtu.be/_UoMXF73j0c.

3. Ed Mylett, *Performance and Mastery in Sports and Life—Interview with Alan Stein, Jr on How to Crush the Game*, YouTube, June 14, 2022, https://youtu.be /DU6ncc8hM6w.

Chapter 12

1. Simon Sinek, *How Great Leaders Inspire Action*, TEDxPuget Sound, September 29, 2009, https://www.ted.com/talks/simon_sinek_how_great_leaders_inspire _action.

2. Lynda Katz Wilner, *Do You Speak Too Fast or Too S-L-O-W-L-Y?*, July 4, 2016, https://successfully-speaking.com/blog/2016/6/27/do-you-speak-toofast-or -toooo-s-l-o-w-l-y.

3. Vanessa Van Edwards, *Cues: Master the Secret Language of Charismatic Communication* (New York: Portfolio/Penguin, 2022).

Index

About the Authors

 **Anne Bruce** doesn't just present for a living, she's also a popular talent manager and a global speaker/author coach and mentor. She's been helping celebrities, politicians, sports figures, and well-known business leaders soar to the next level of their career, as well as helping up-and-coming presenters learn the ropes and refine their skills.

Anne has spoken, written, and conducted talent projects across the globe for Accenture, the American Red Cross, Baylor University Medical Center, Ben & Jerry's, Coca-Cola, Columbia University School of Business, the Conference Board of Europe, the FBI, GEICO, Harvard Law School, JetBlue, NASA (where she produced a documentary on the lives of women astronauts), the Pentagon, Saks Fifth Avenue, Sony Entertainment, Sony International, Southwest Airlines, Stanford Law School, and the White House.

With a background in broadcast journalism and television work, Anne has written for clients and projects from Hollywood to New York. Her clients have appeared on, and she has written for guests and producers of *Shark Tank*, *Steve Harvey*, *Today Show*, *Good Morning America*, *Anderson Cooper 360°*, *The View*, CNN, *CBS Evening News*, *48 Hours*, and numerous newspapers, magazine, online news outlets, and more. She's also carved a niche in coaching talent to write and deliver popular TEDx and TED Talks.

She is the author of dozens of books and numerous e-books, which have been translated into more than 40 languages worldwide. Some of Anne's books include *Speak for a Living: The Insider's Guide to Building a Speaking Career, Second Edition*; *Discover True North: A 4-Week Program to Ignite Your Passion and Activate Your Potential*; *Be Your Own Mentor*; *Motivating Employees, 2nd Edition*; *How to Motivate Every Employee*; and *Building a High Morale Workplace*. She is an author in McGraw Hill's popular *Perfect Phrases* series and *Mighty Manager* series. She has been interviewed by the *Wall Street Journal*, *The Times* (London), *San Jose Mercury News*, *Newsweek*, *Inc.*, and *Entrepreneur*, among others.

Anne's home base is in the greater Los Angeles area at Channel Islands Beach—also her favorite place to coach clients and film her popular video blog, #30SecondsAtTheBeach. She has also partnered with her coauthor, Sardék Love, to launch the Speak for a Living Success Academy, a program for aspiring and accomplished speakers. Learn more about it at www.speakforalivingsuccessacademy.com.

Anne wants to hear from you! Connect with her and share your stories of life on the speaker circuit on Facebook (Fans of Anne Bruce), Instagram (@annebruceauthor), LinkedIn (Anne Bruce), TikTok (@annebruceauthor), Twitter (@TrueNorthAuthor), and YouTube (Anne Bruce), and as well as www.AnneBruce.com. DM Anne or email her to request a 30-minute complimentary coaching session at Anne@AnneBruce.com.

Sardék Love is a peak performance and employee engagement expert who equips leaders and talent development professionals with the systems and tools for creating high-performing teams that deliver predictable performance and profitable results. As a master trainer, keynote speaker, and master performance consultant, he has worked in 32 countries spanning Europe, the Middle East, North America, Latin America, and Southeast Asia.

Sardék has had the honor of speaking, training, and consulting for leading organizations, including Abbott Laboratories, the Association for Talent Development (ATD), AstraZeneca, Audi of America, Chevron, Orangetheory Fitness, Procter & Gamble, Ritz-Carlton, and more. As a leading global expert in training and development, he has authored several blog articles published by ATD and is coauthor of *Maintaining Cohesiveness in a Distributed Government Workforce*, part of the *TD at Work* series. Sardék is the creator of the Facilitating with Impact! System, a leading facilitation and training delivery model used by training professionals worldwide.

He is a highly sought-after international keynote speaker. His signature program, which is composed of his "Leading with Impact" series of speeches, is a favorite among leaders and has been delivered to organizations such as Brooks Rehabilitation, Broward Health, Daxko, US Department of Housing and Urban Development, US Senate, and Yazaki Corporation. In partnering with Anne Bruce to write *Presentation Essentials*, Sardék continues to live his life purpose of *Ut Prosim*— "That I May Serve." Connect with and follow Sardék on Facebook (Sardek Love), Instagram (@SardekLove), LinkedIn (Sardek Love), and Twitter (@SardekLove) as well as www.SardekLove.com to receive an endless supply of tools and techniques to take your performance and the performance of your team to the next level.

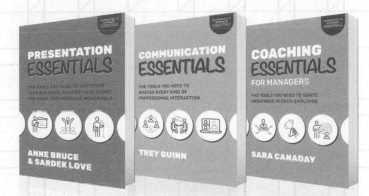